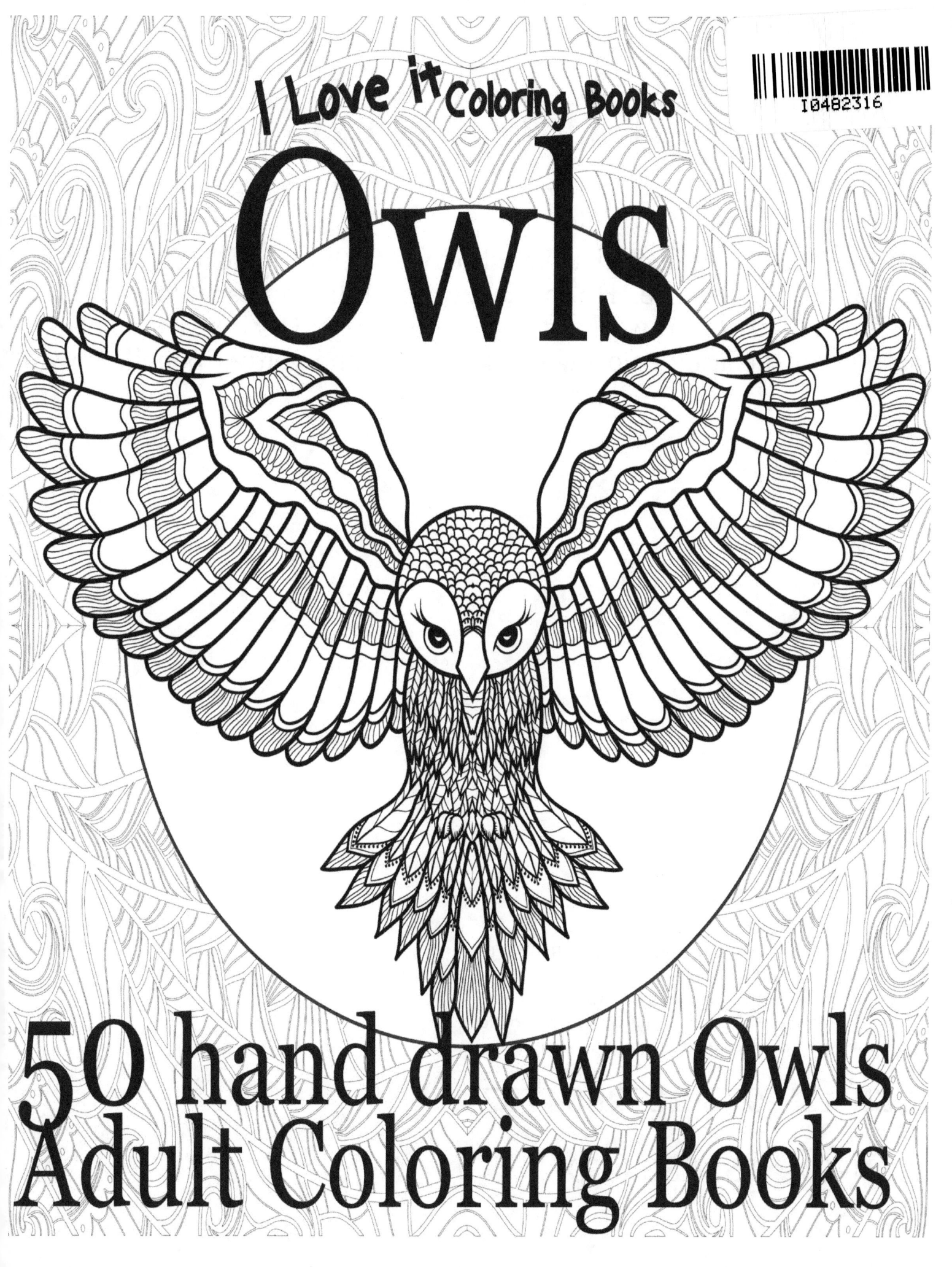

Peter Taylor

Peter Taylor is a talented artist who lives with his wife and 3 children in South West France. He specializes in wildlife ink sketches and has shown many of his works at local exhibitions. His ink sketches are perfect for the adult coloring market, to finish in either pencil, crayon, marker or water colors.

I Love it Coloring Books - An Adult Coloring Books - Owls
By: Peter Taylor - Adult Coloring Books
Copyright Peter Taylor - Images by shutterstock.com

ISBN-13: 978-1532804137

ISBN-10: 153280413X

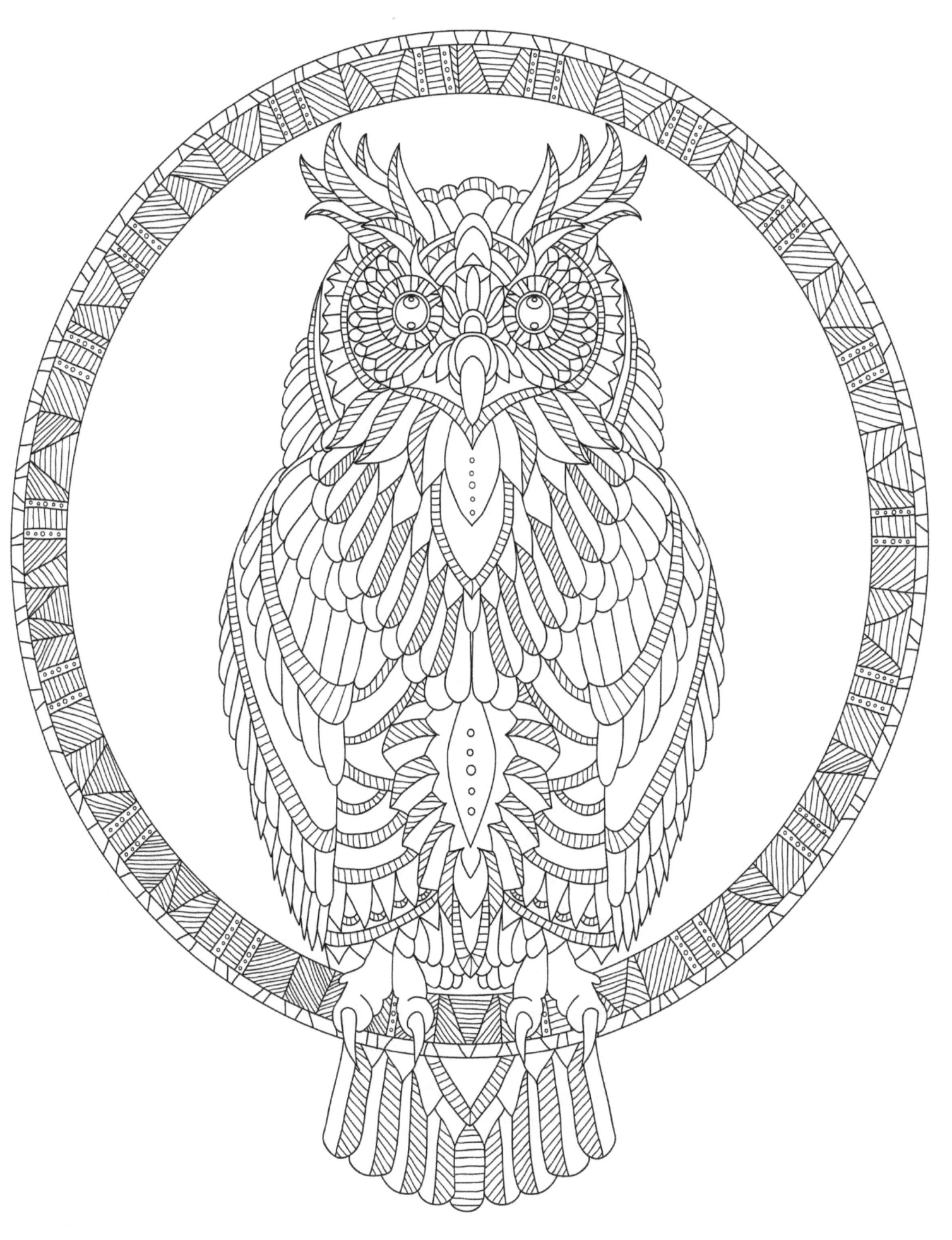

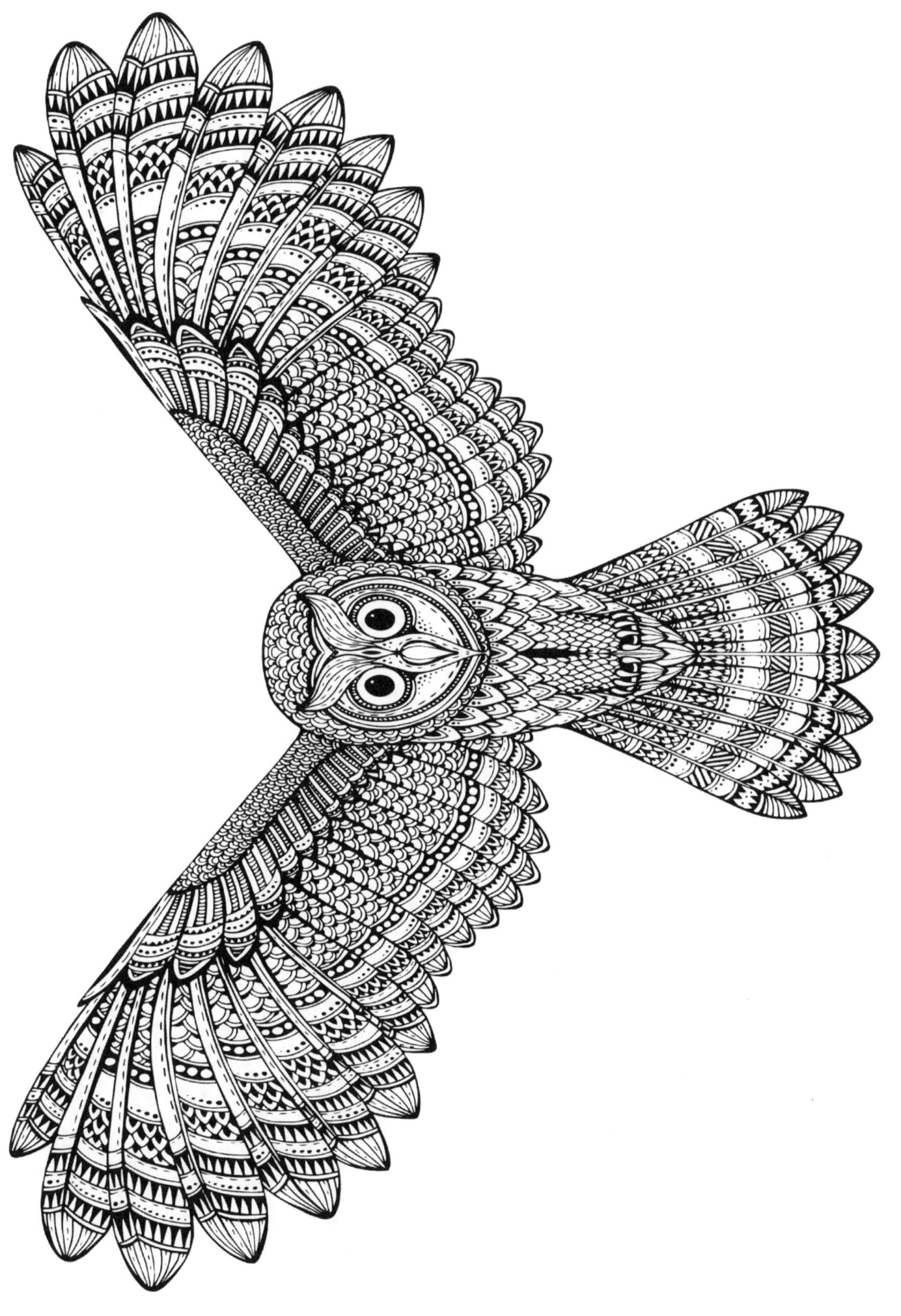

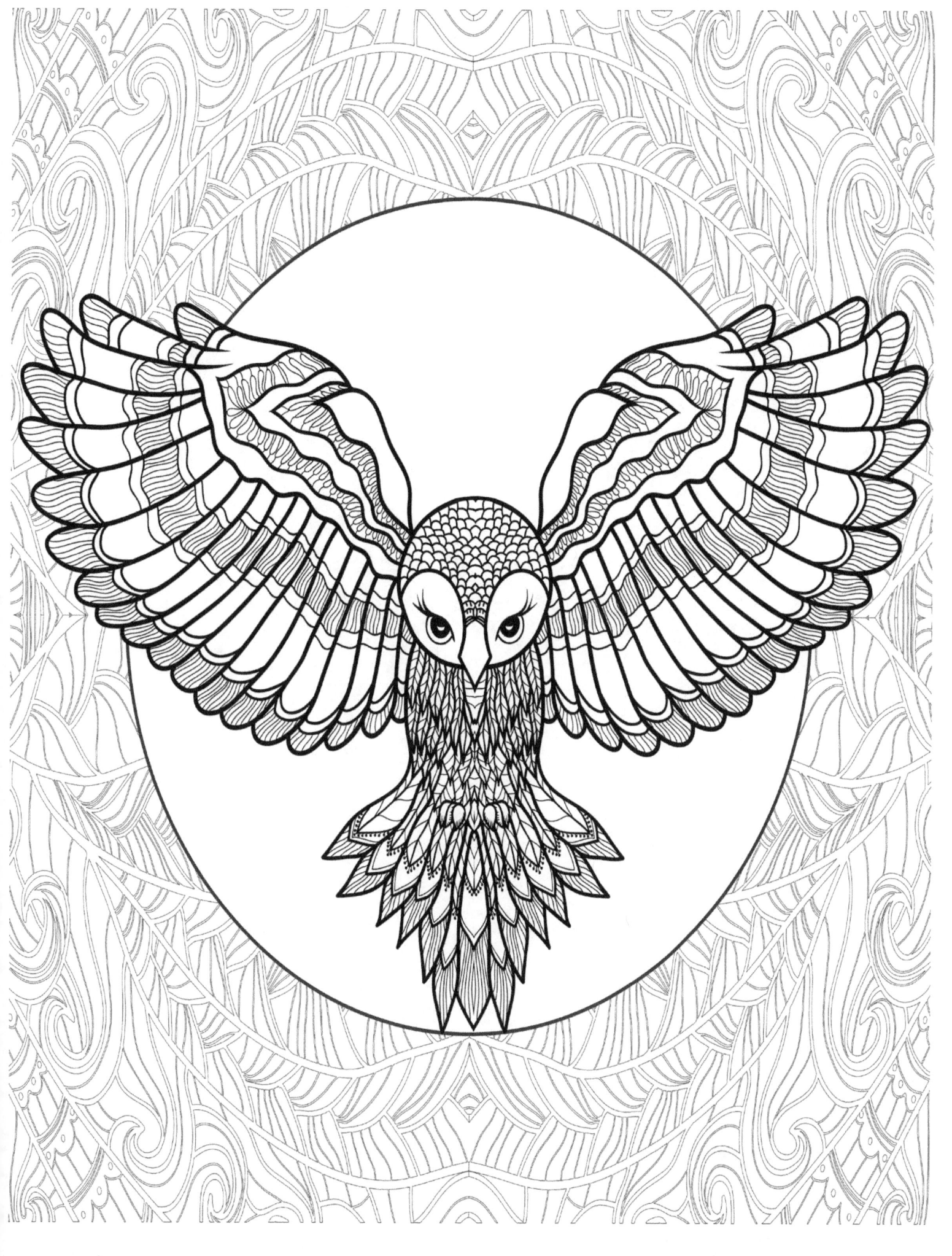

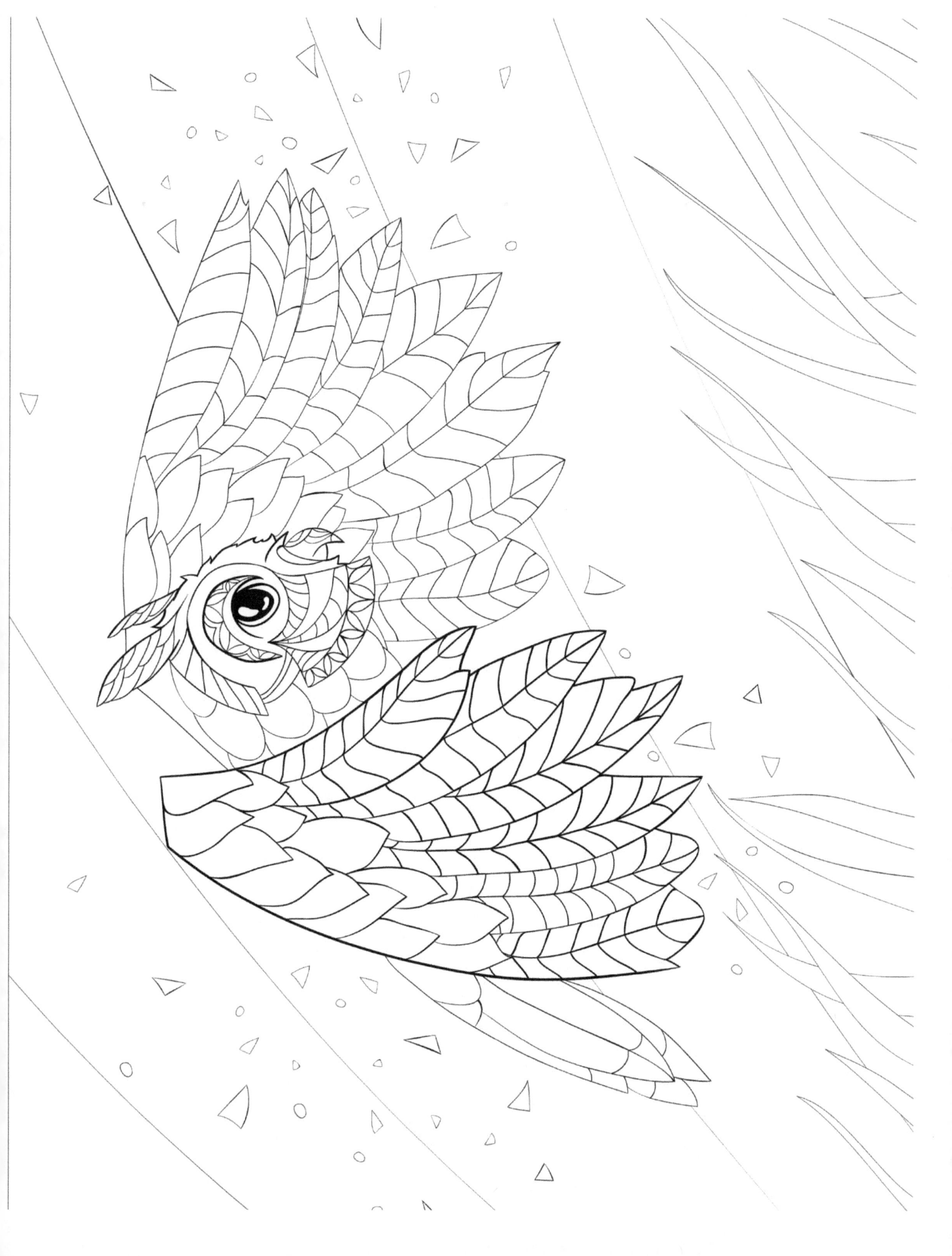

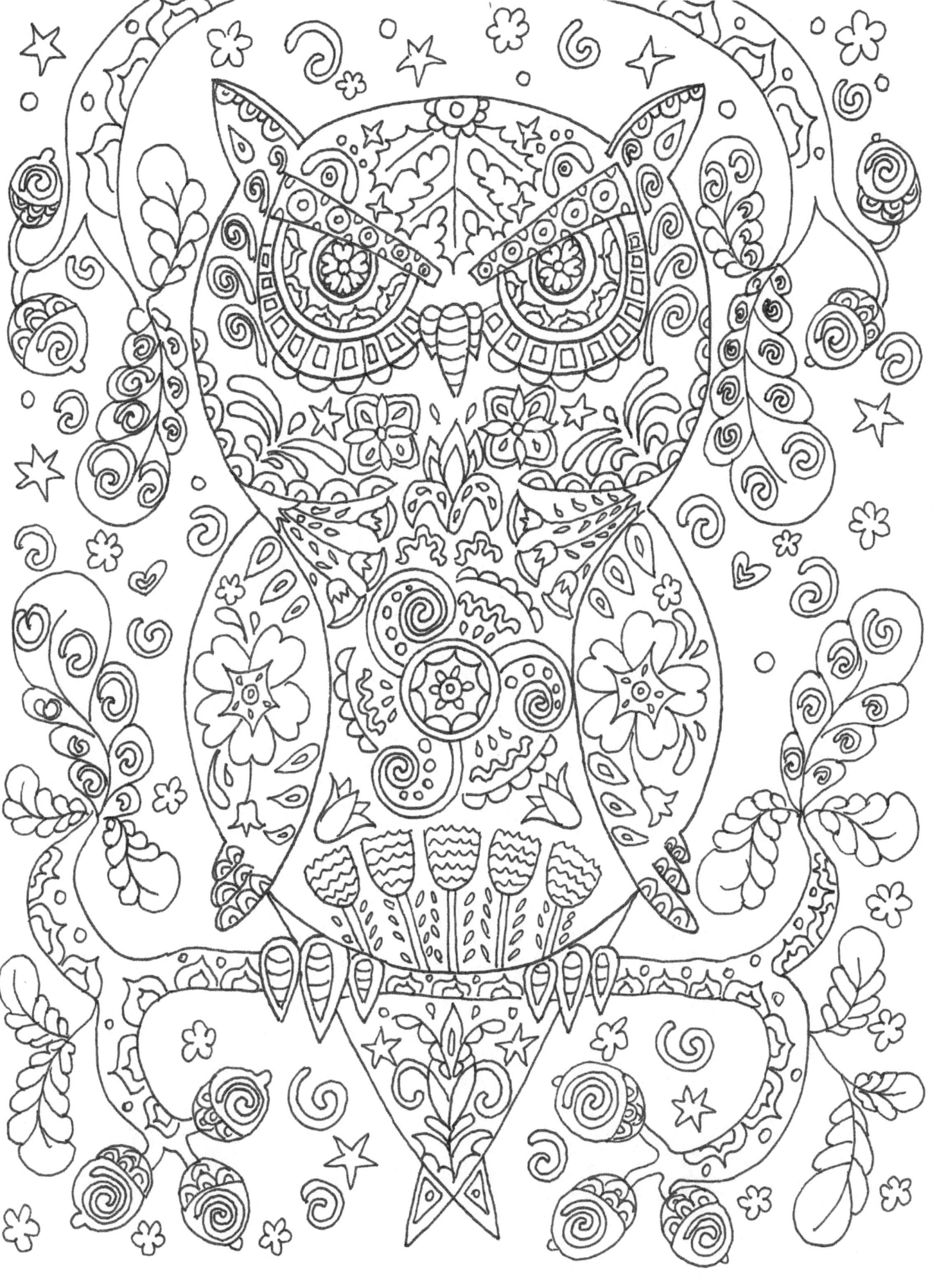

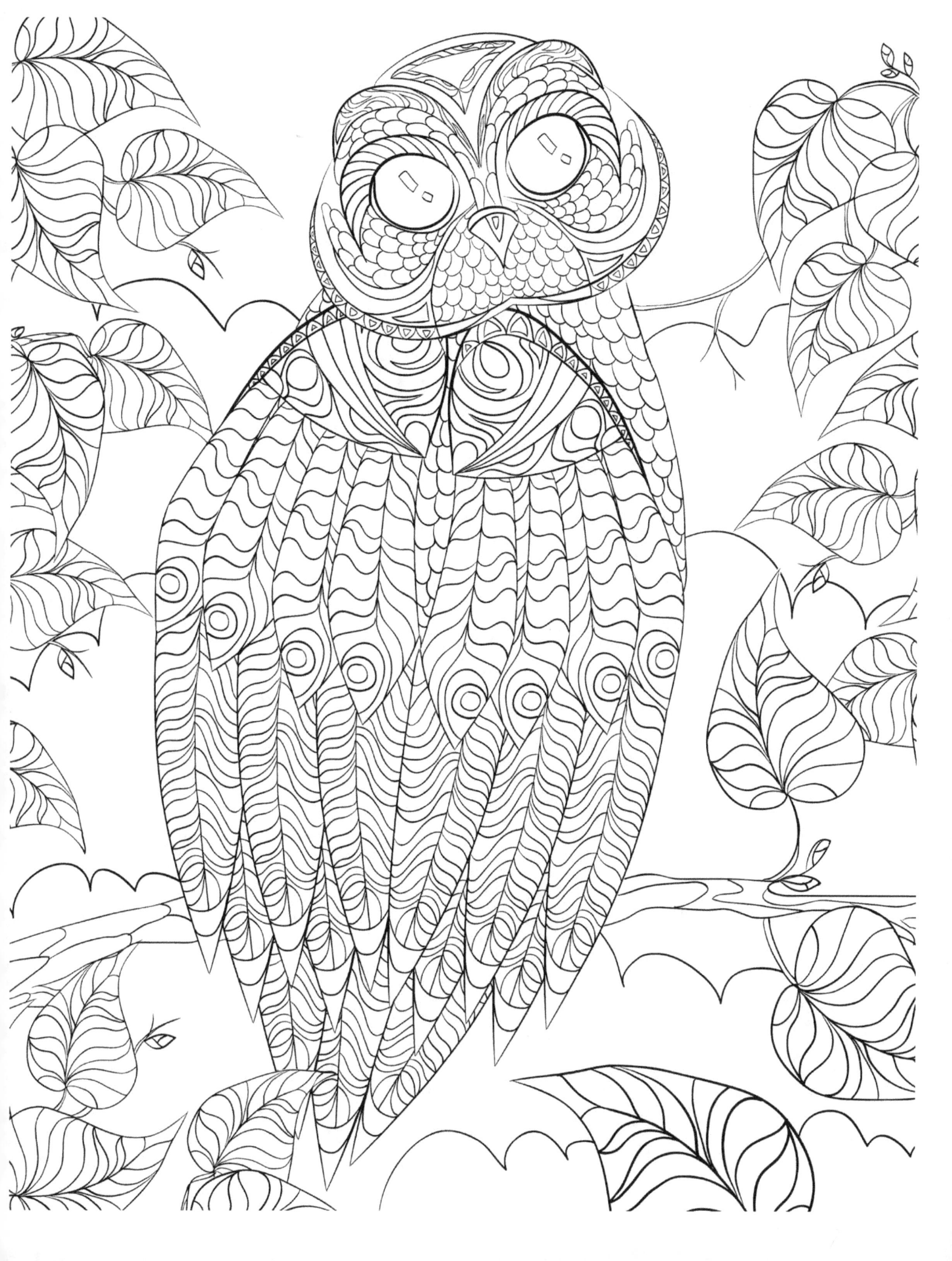

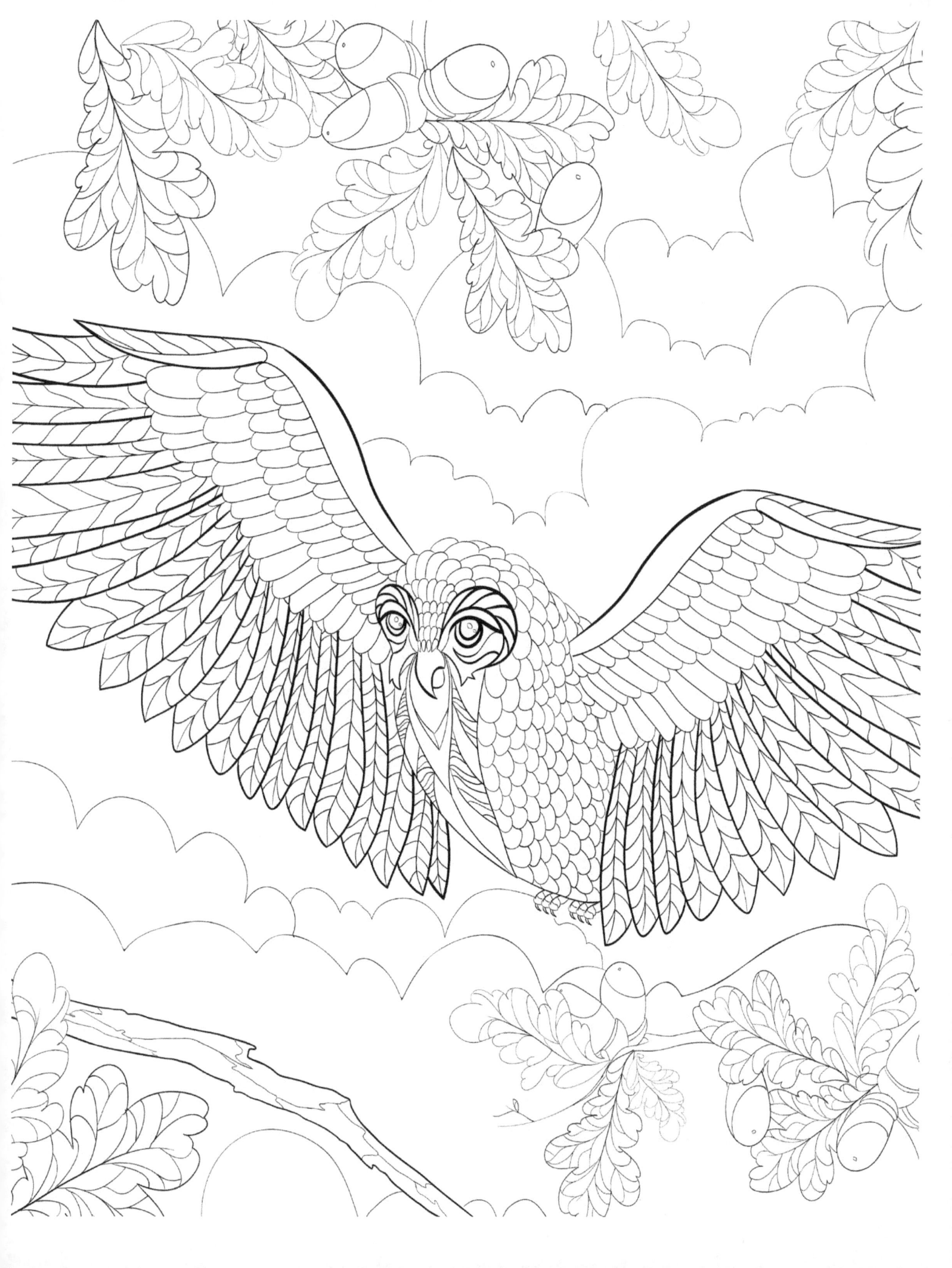

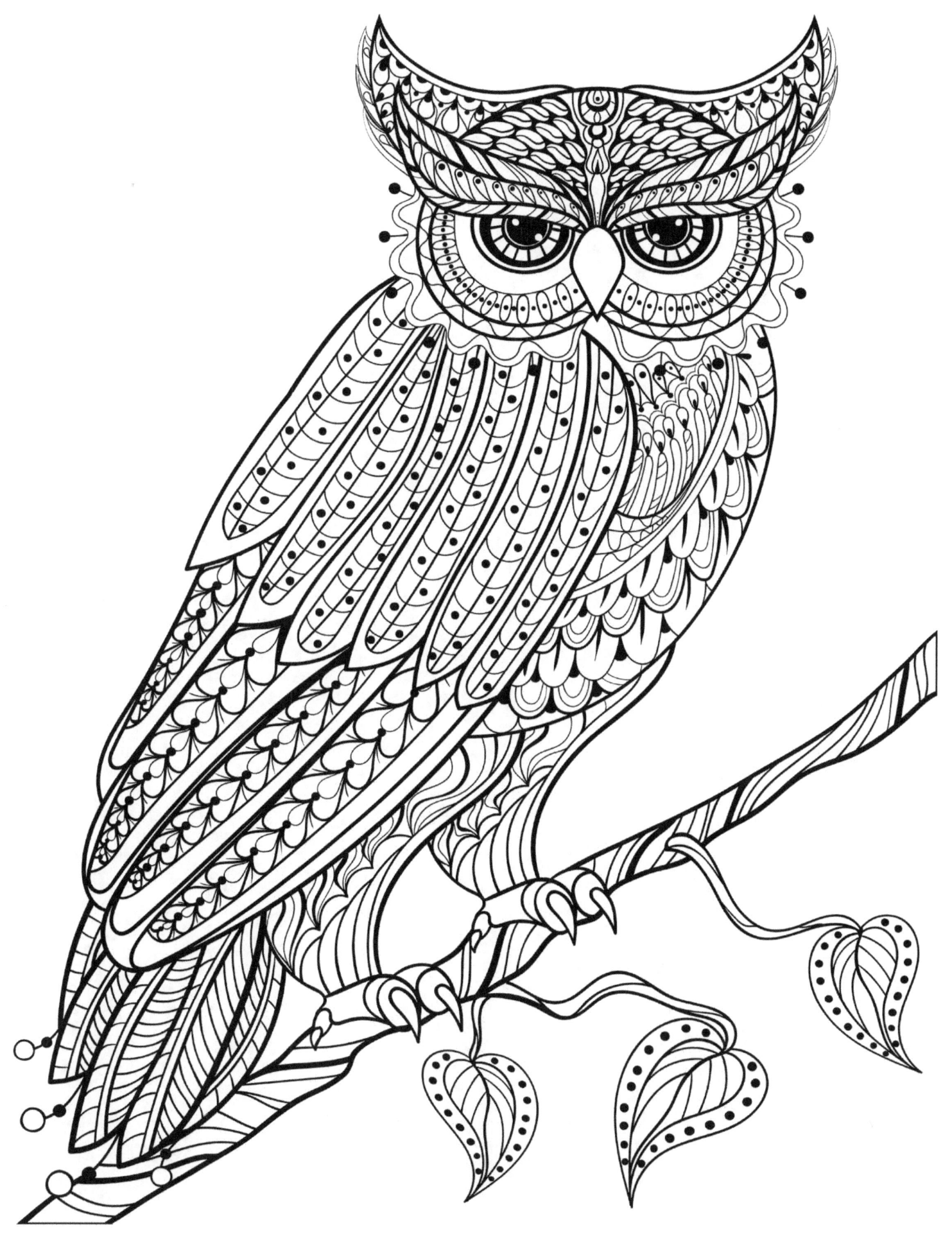

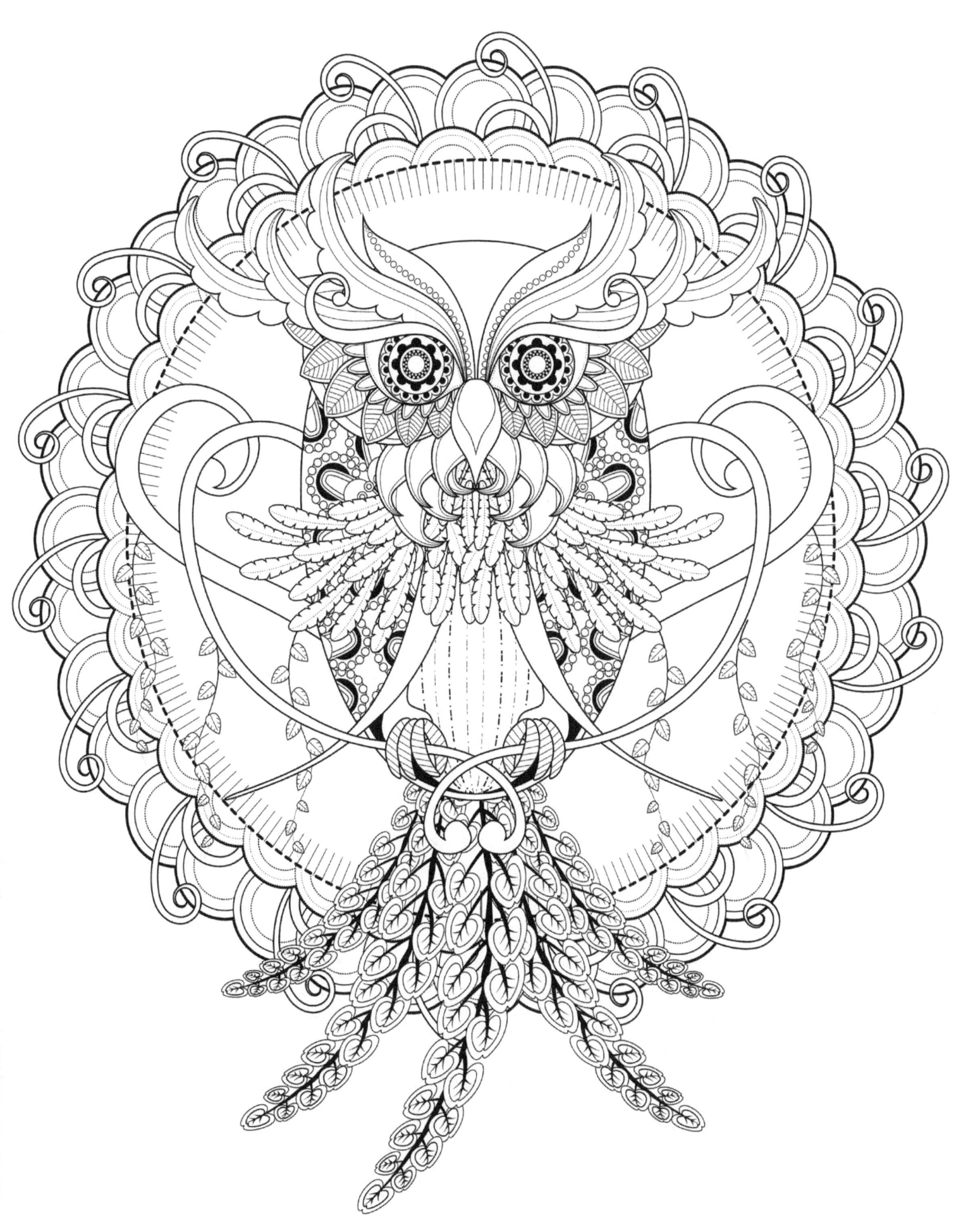

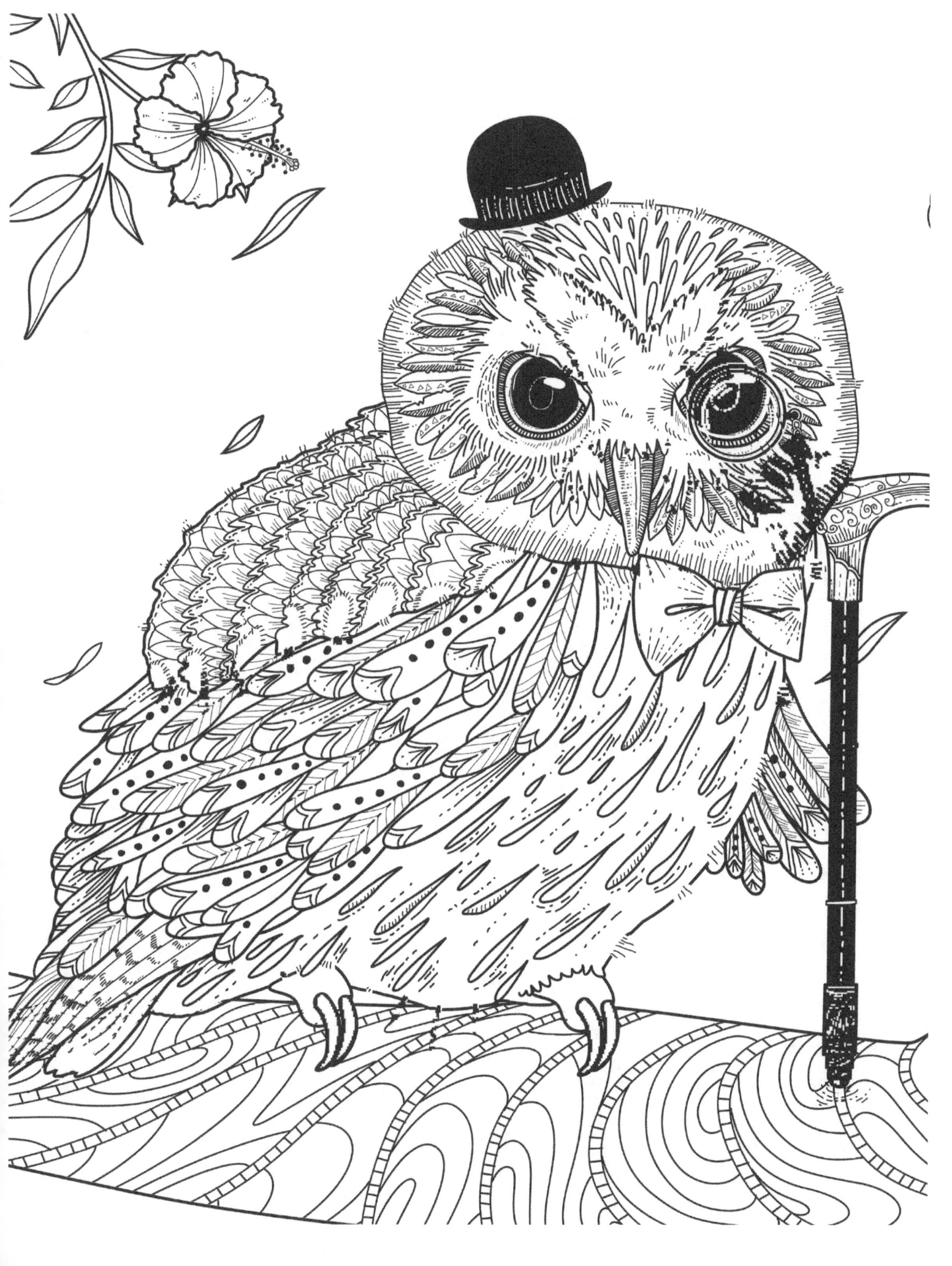

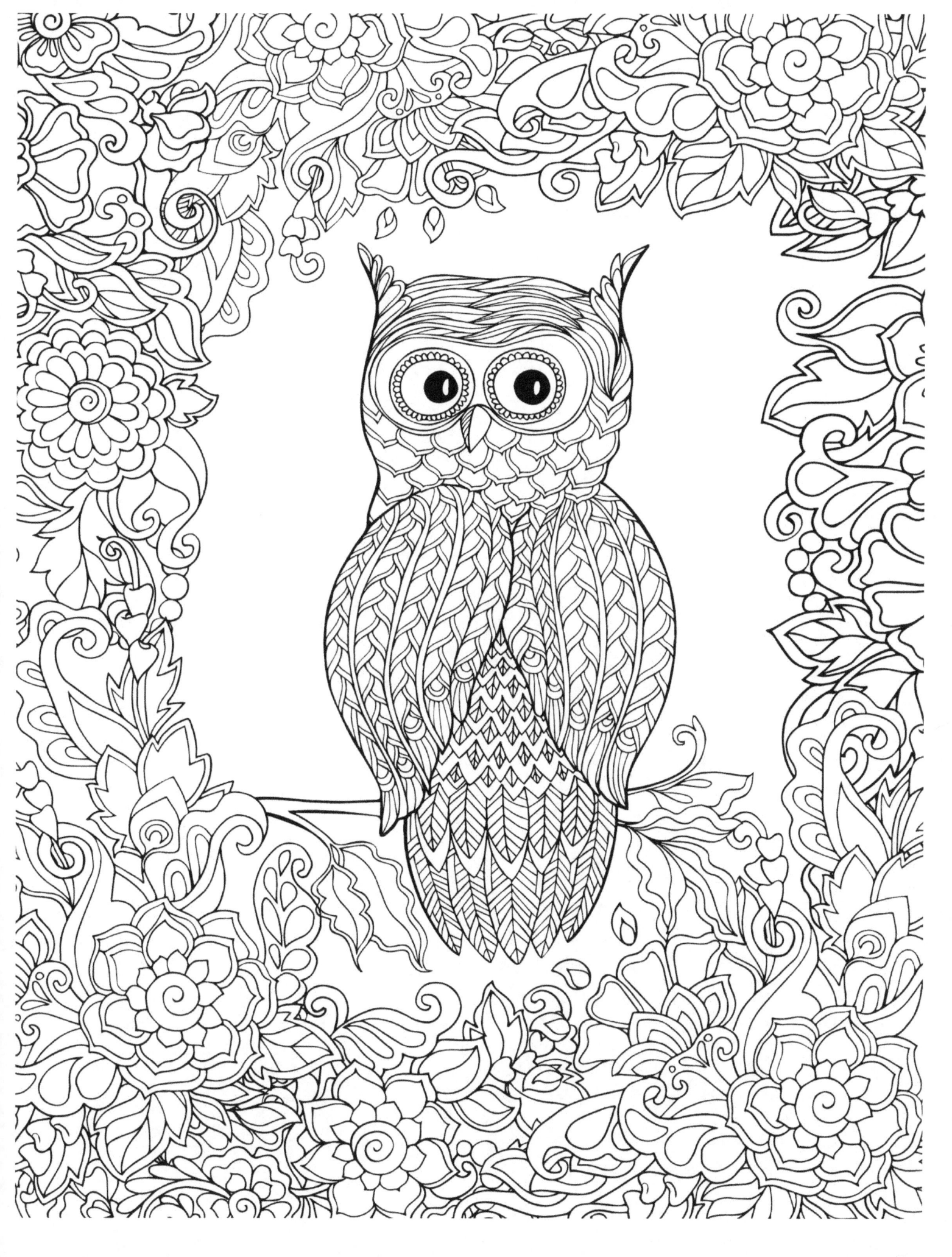

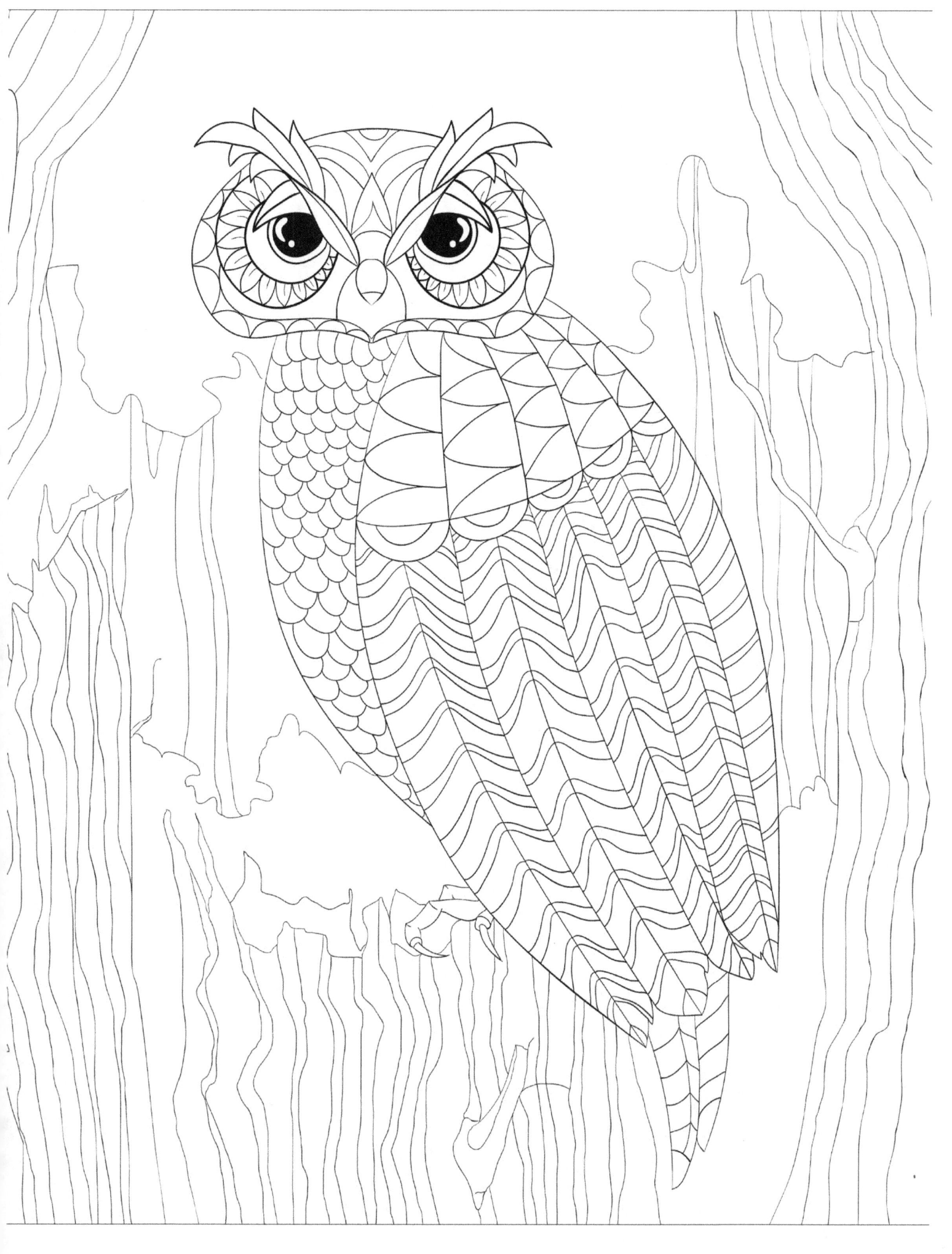

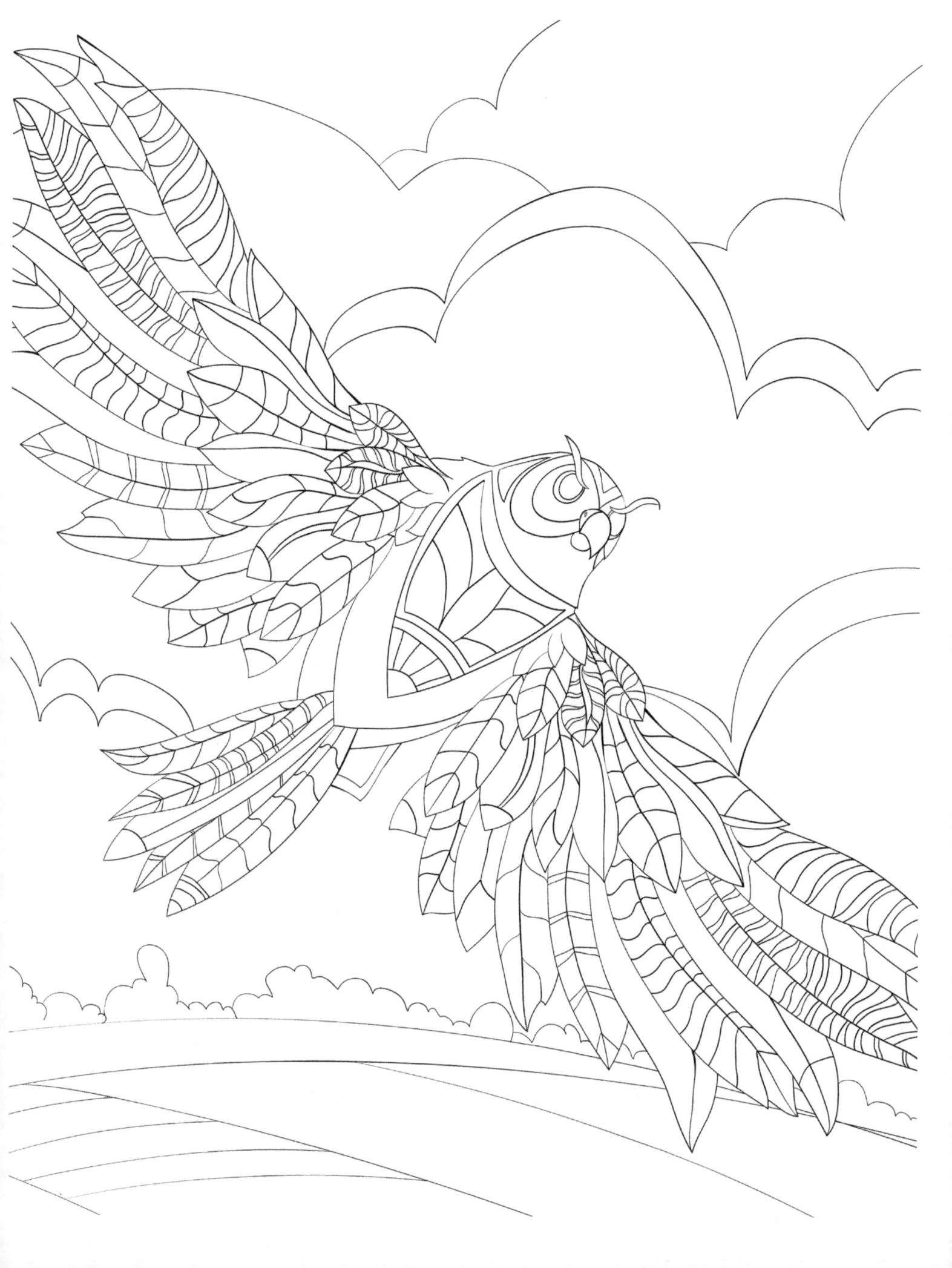

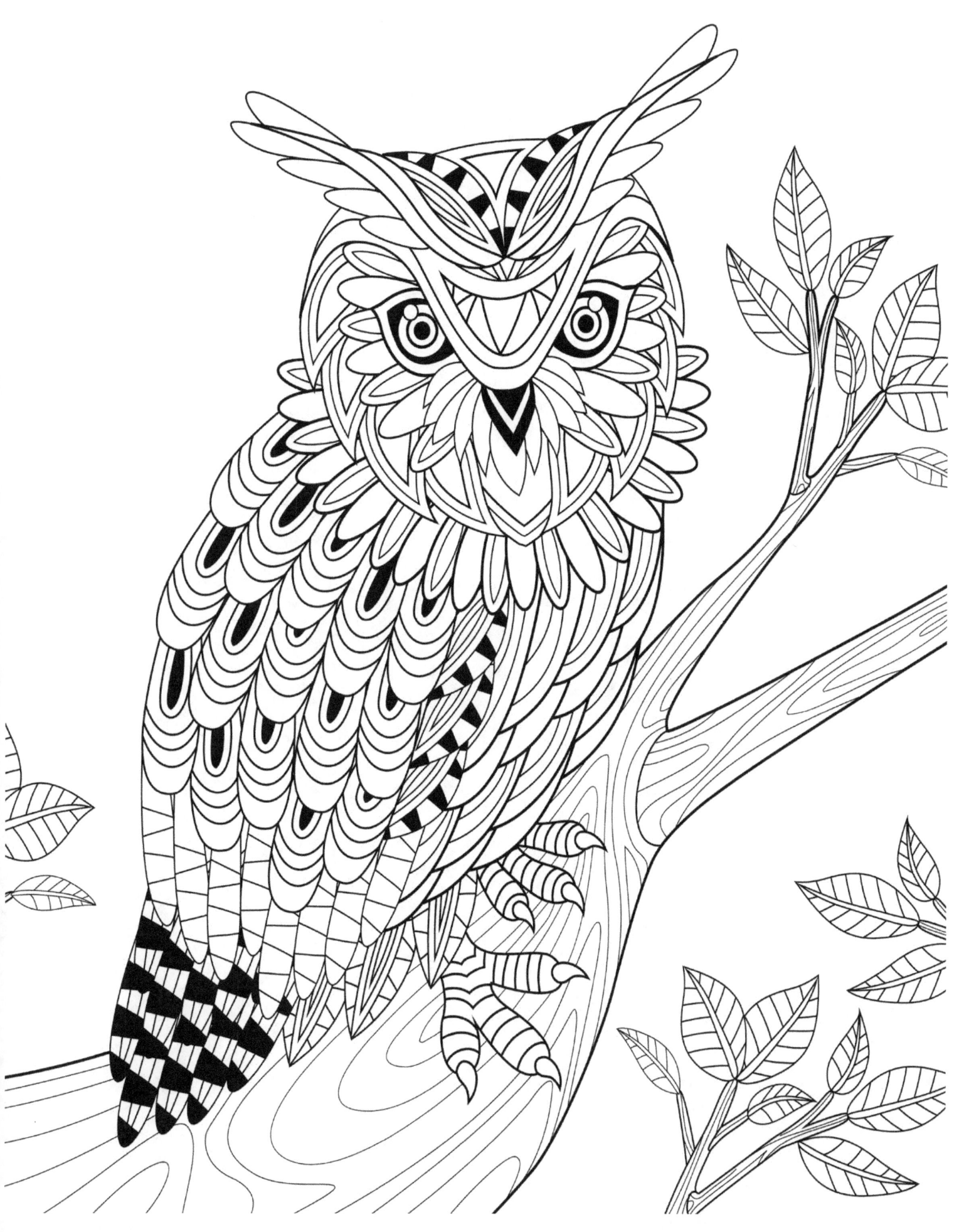

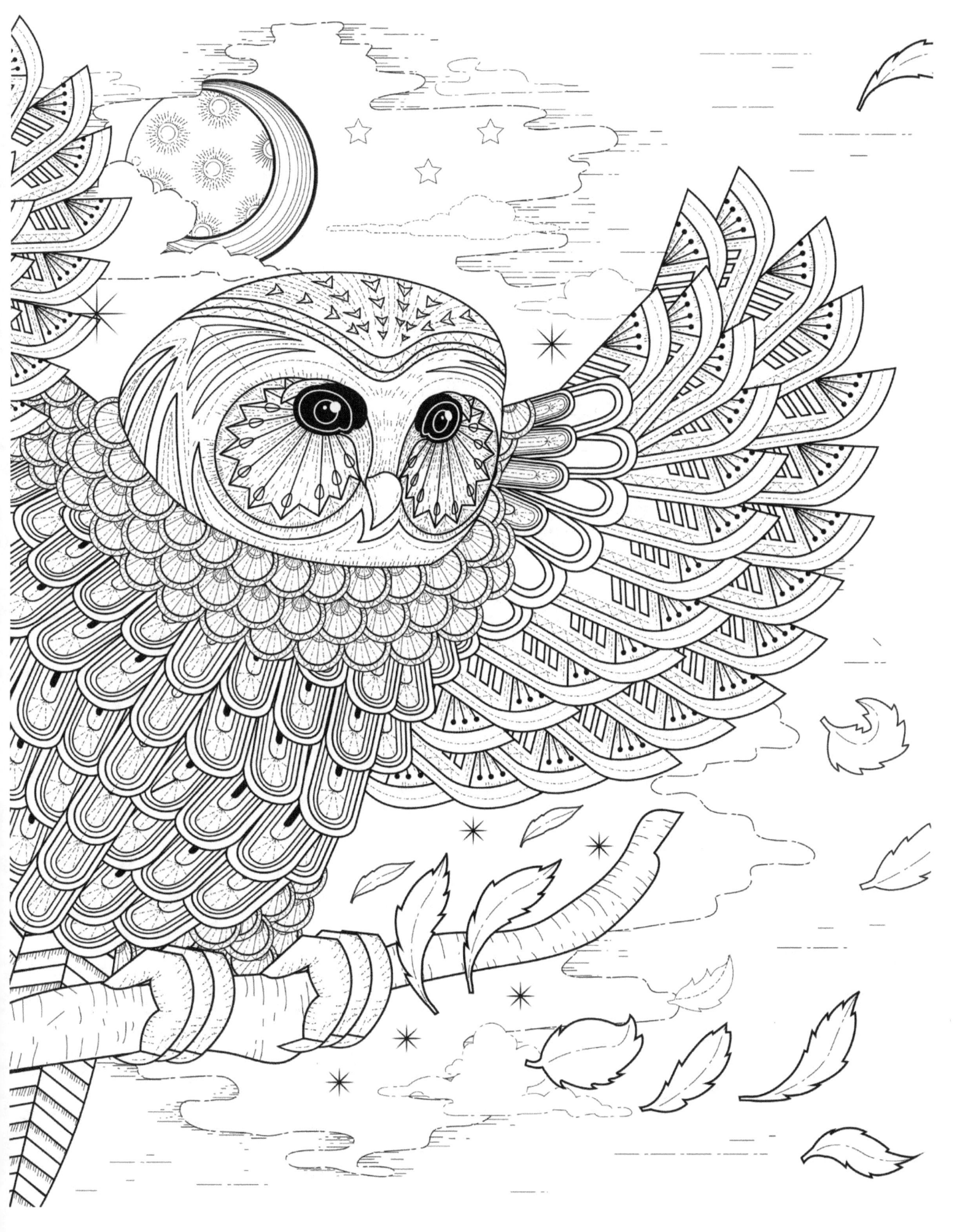

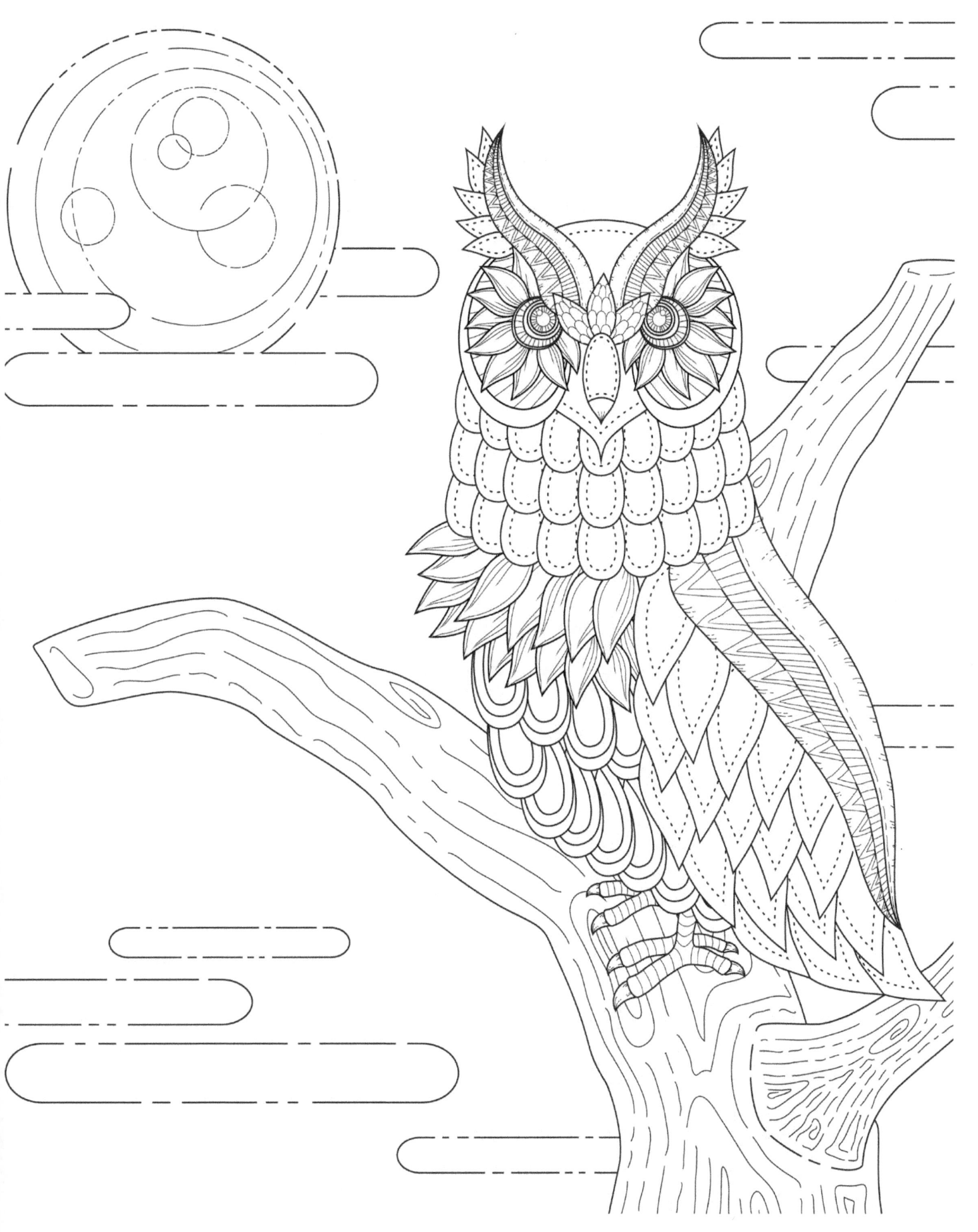

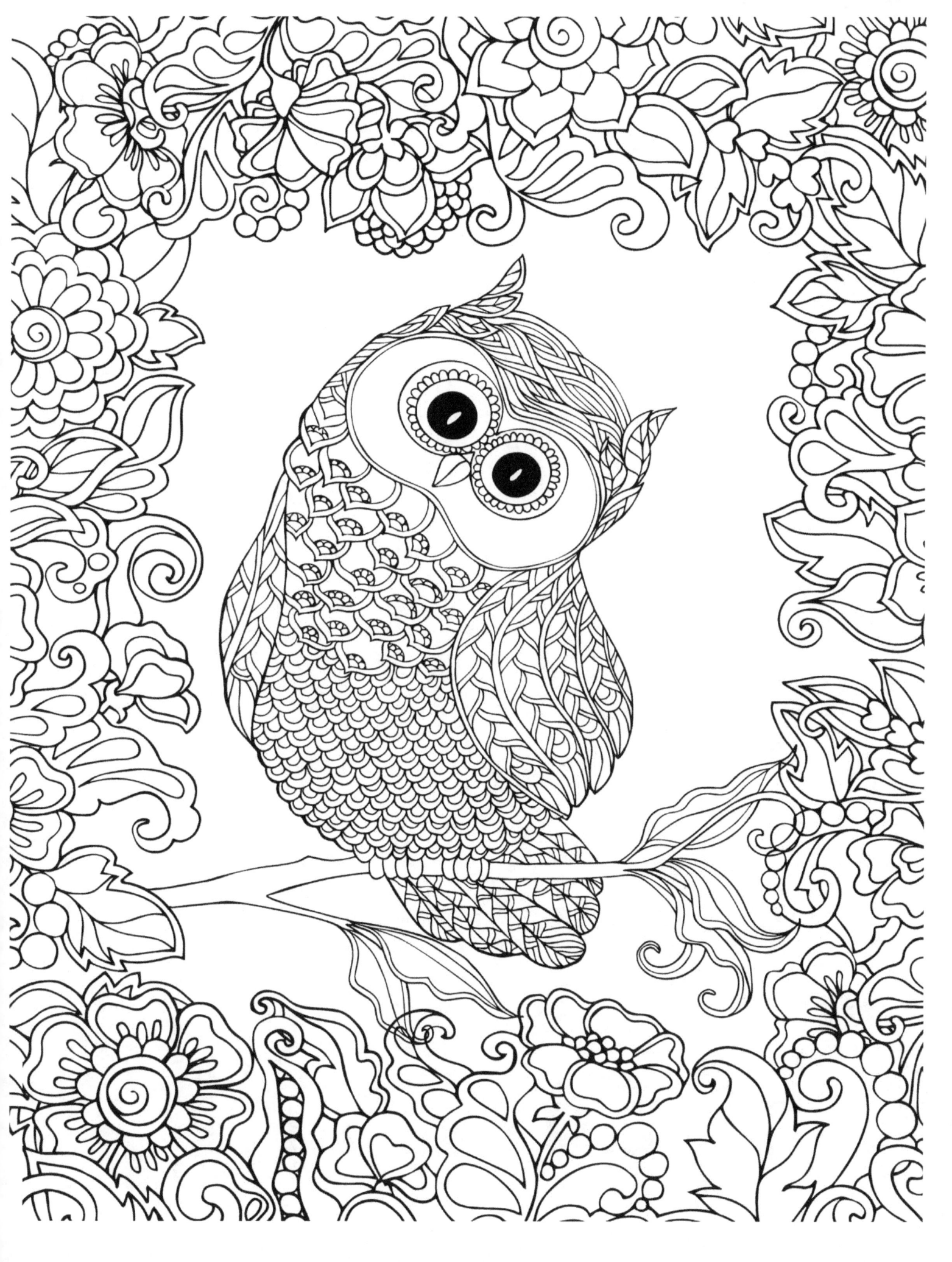

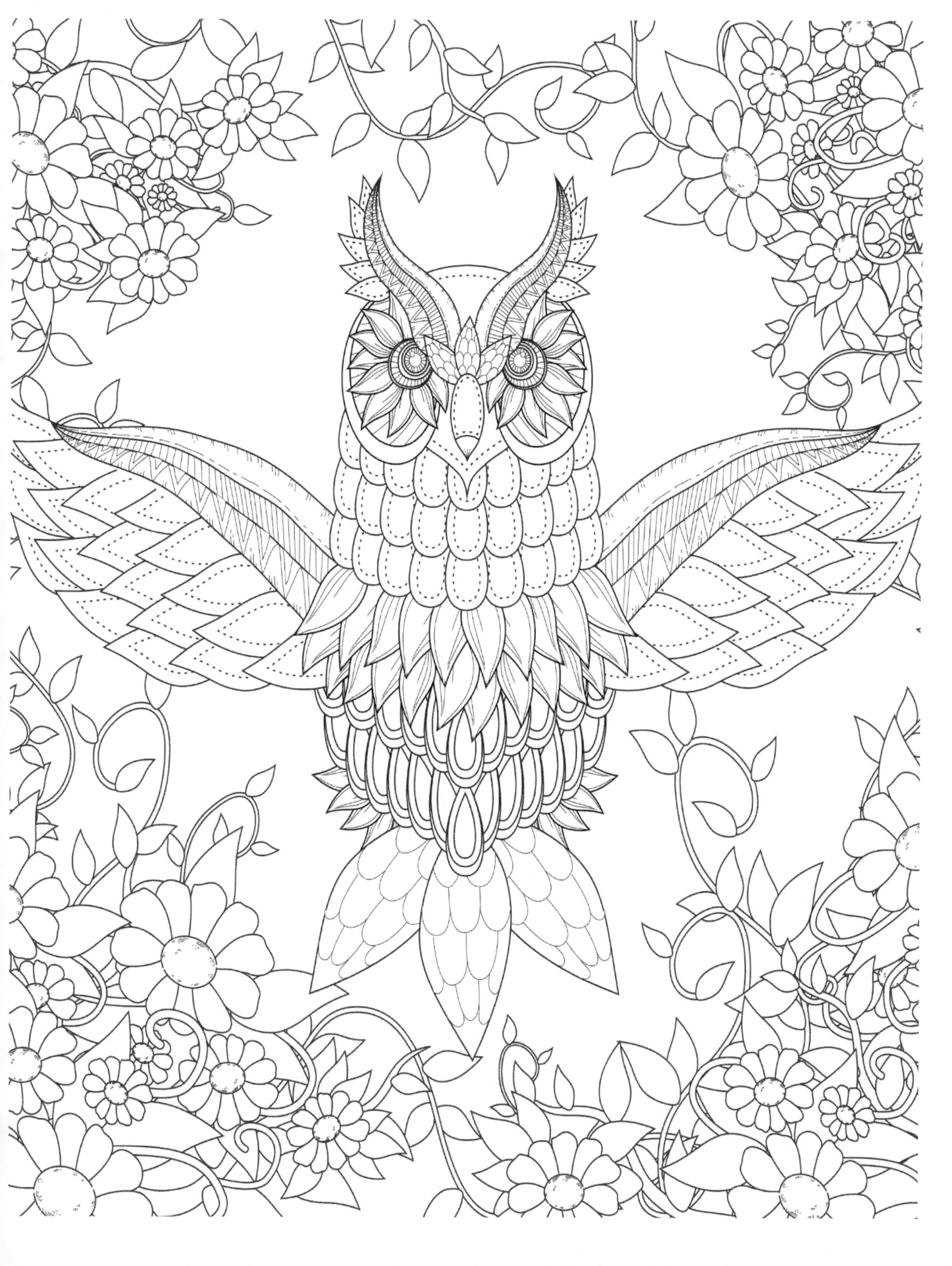

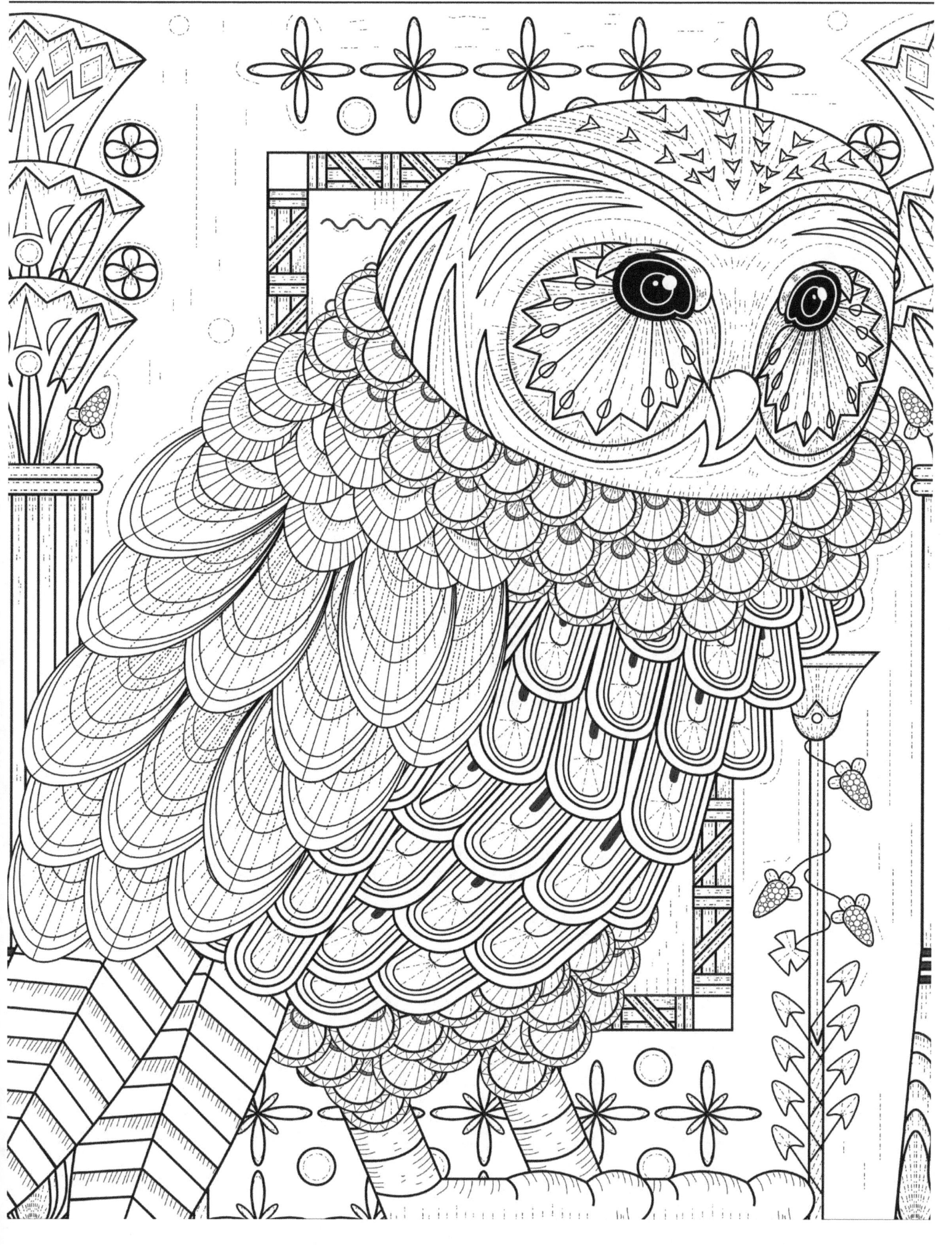

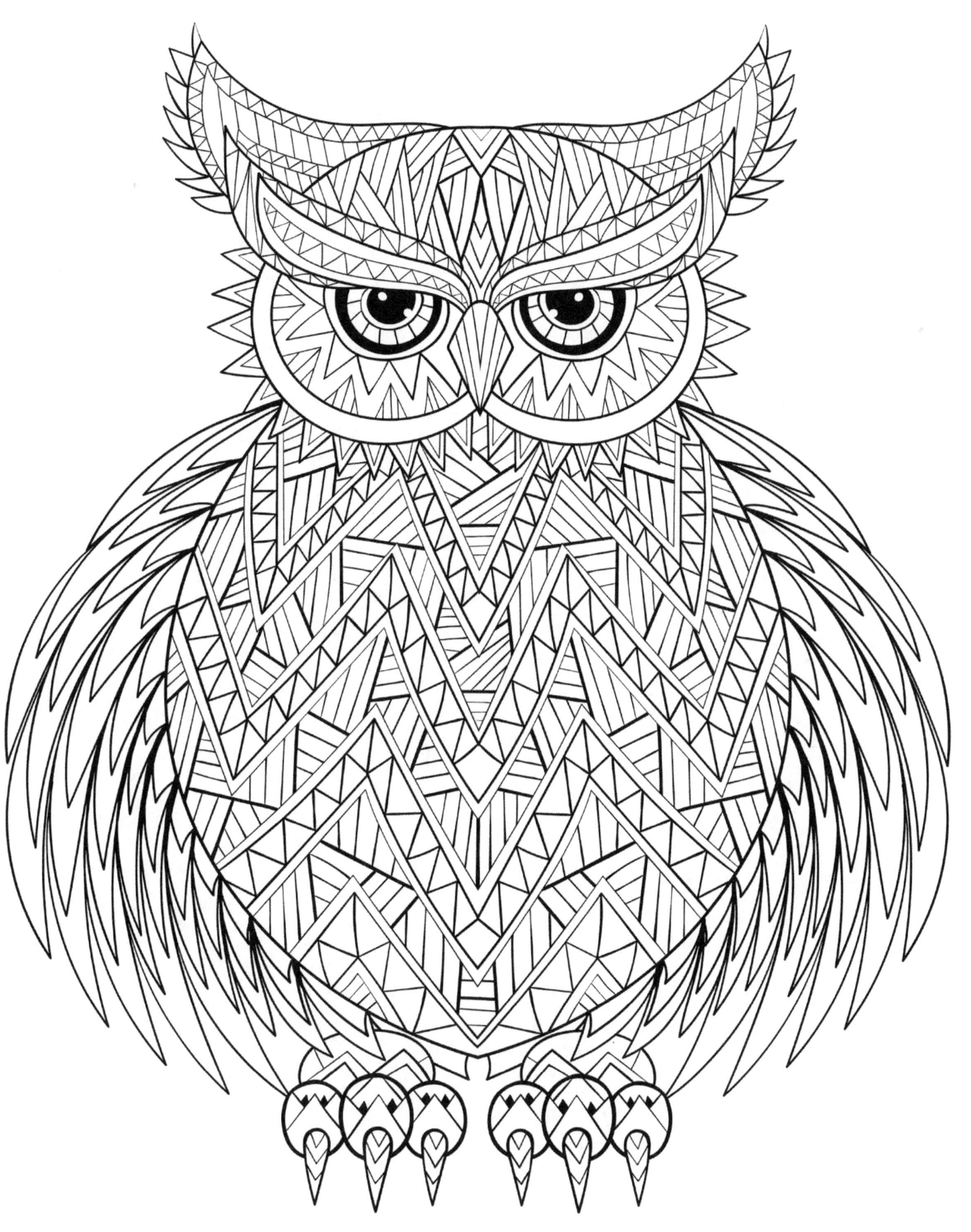

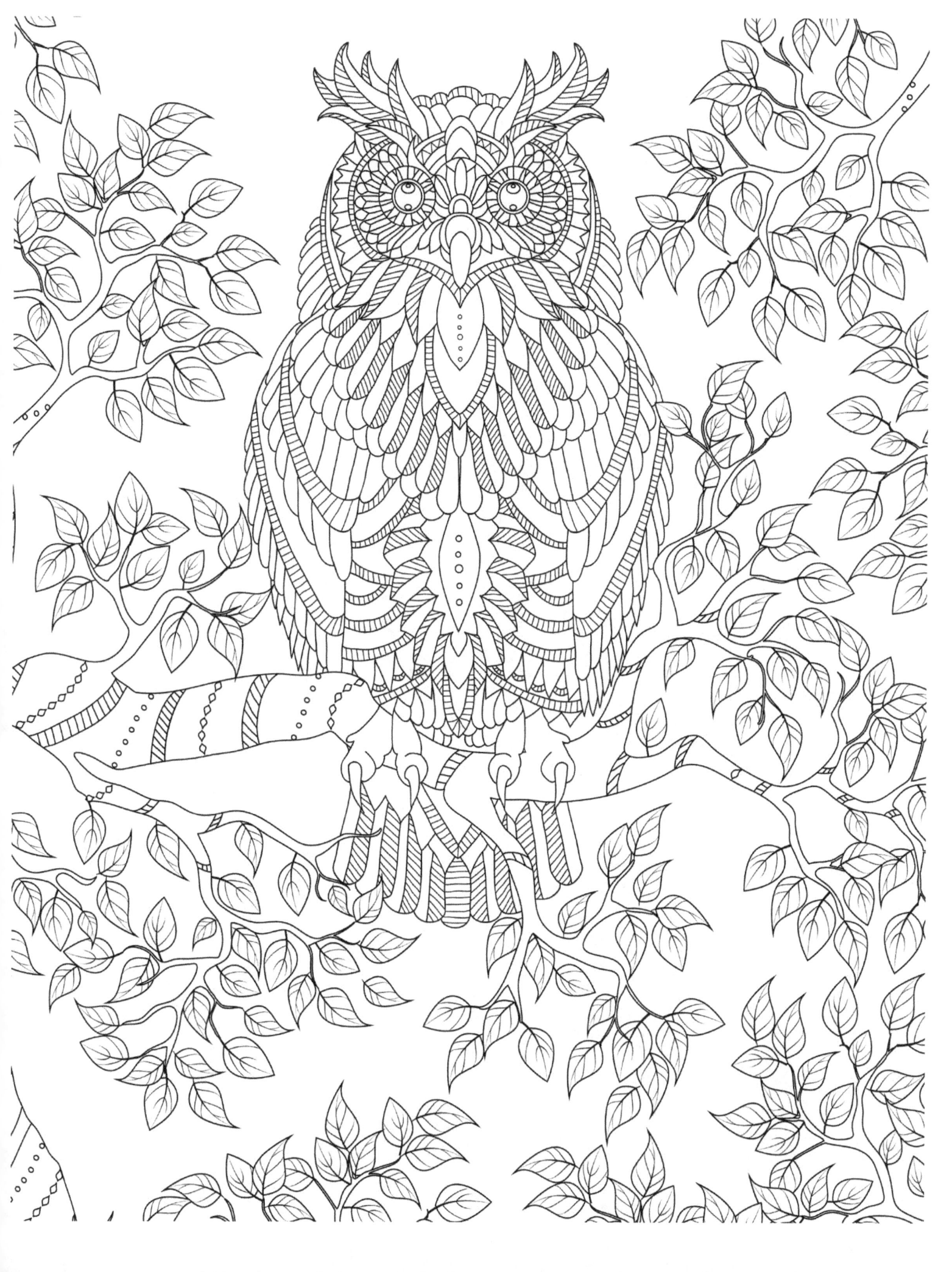

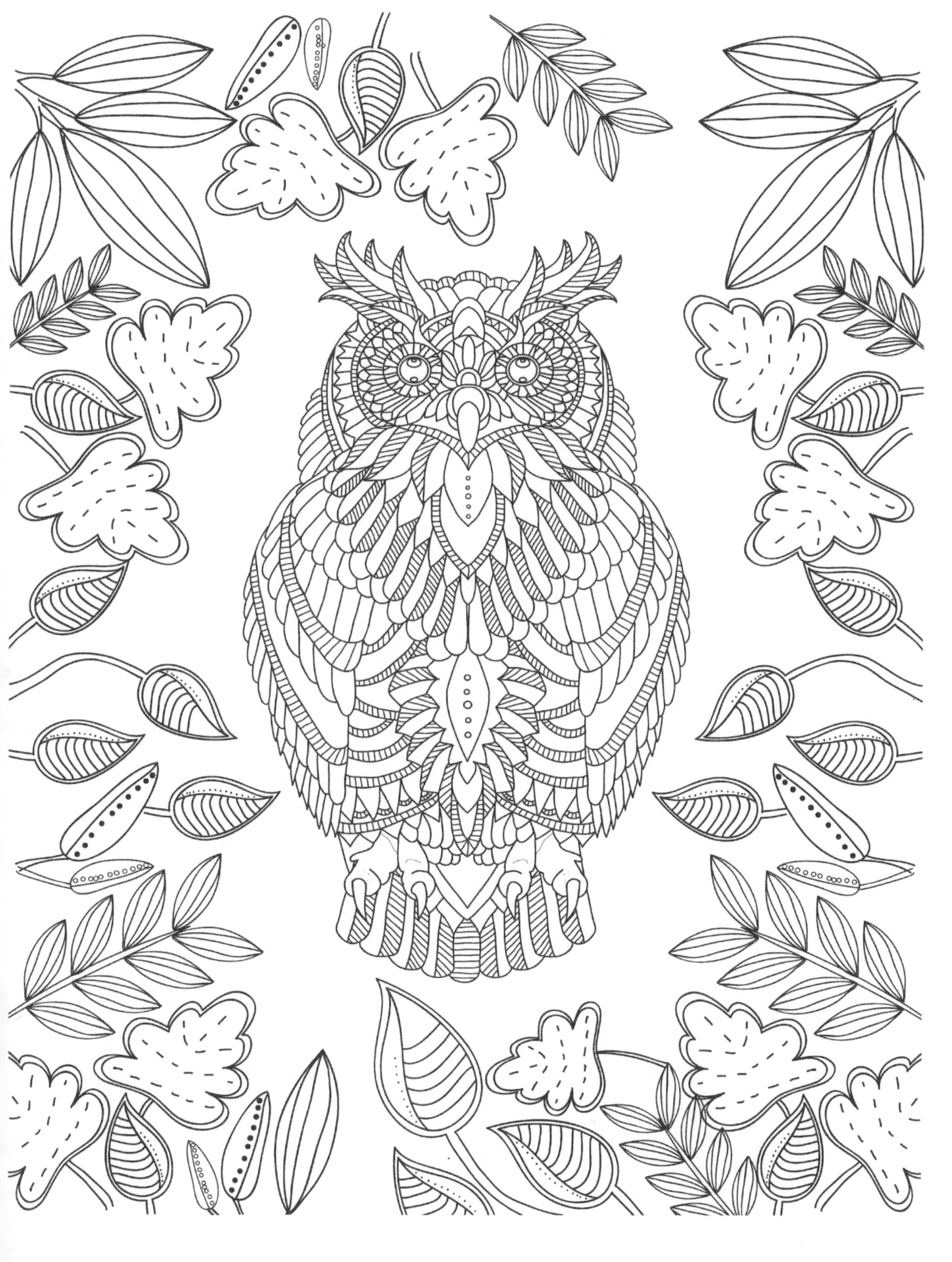

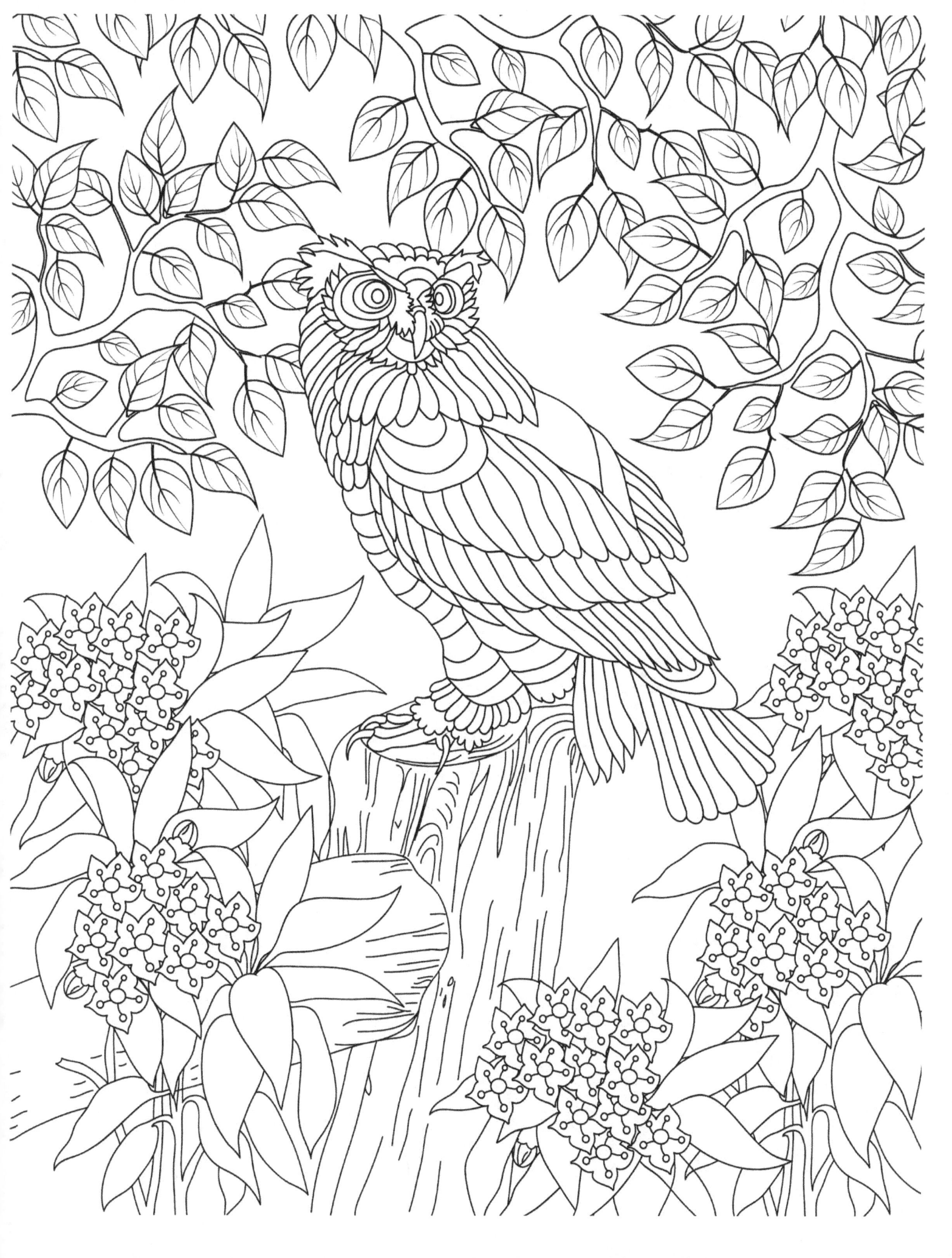

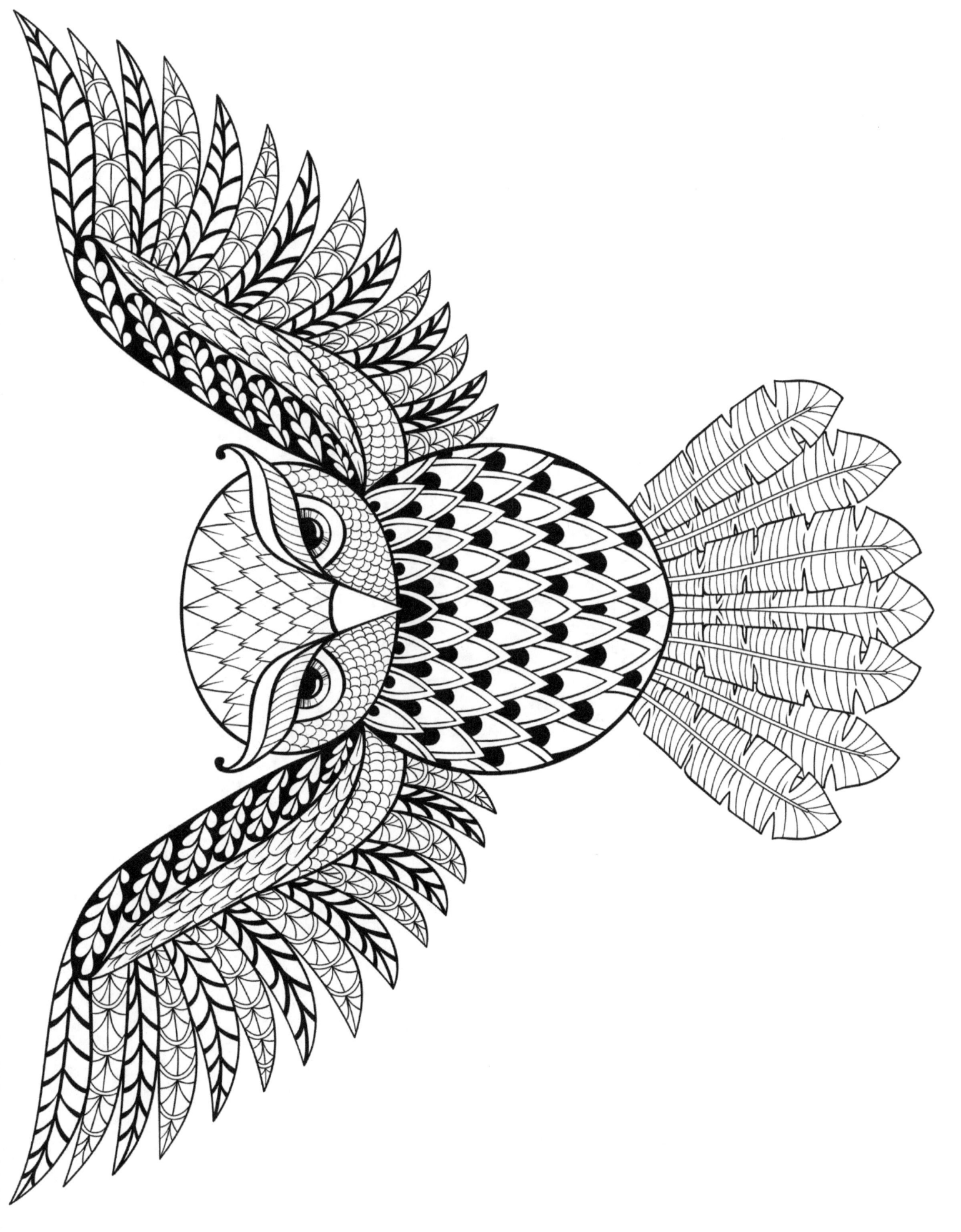

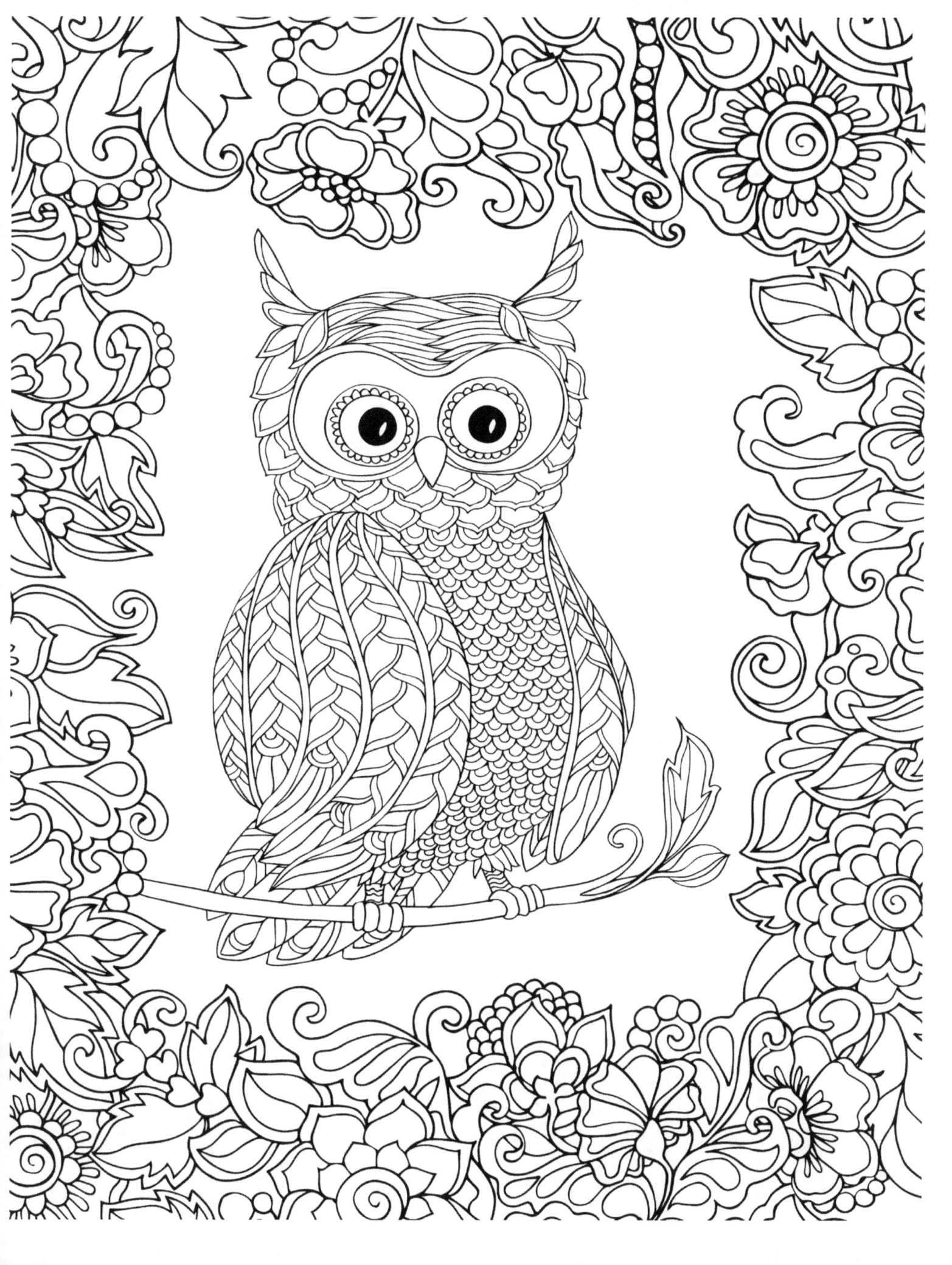

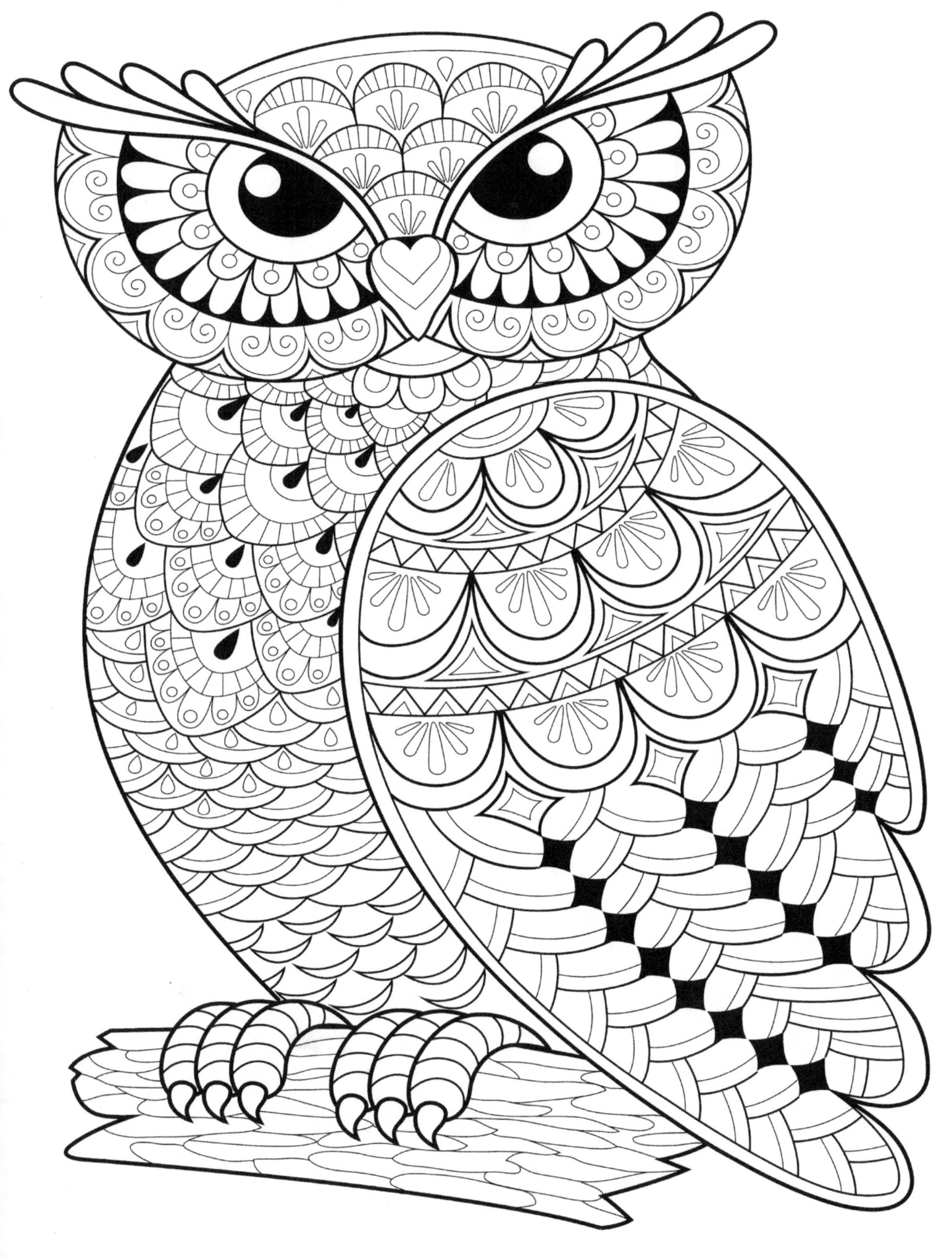

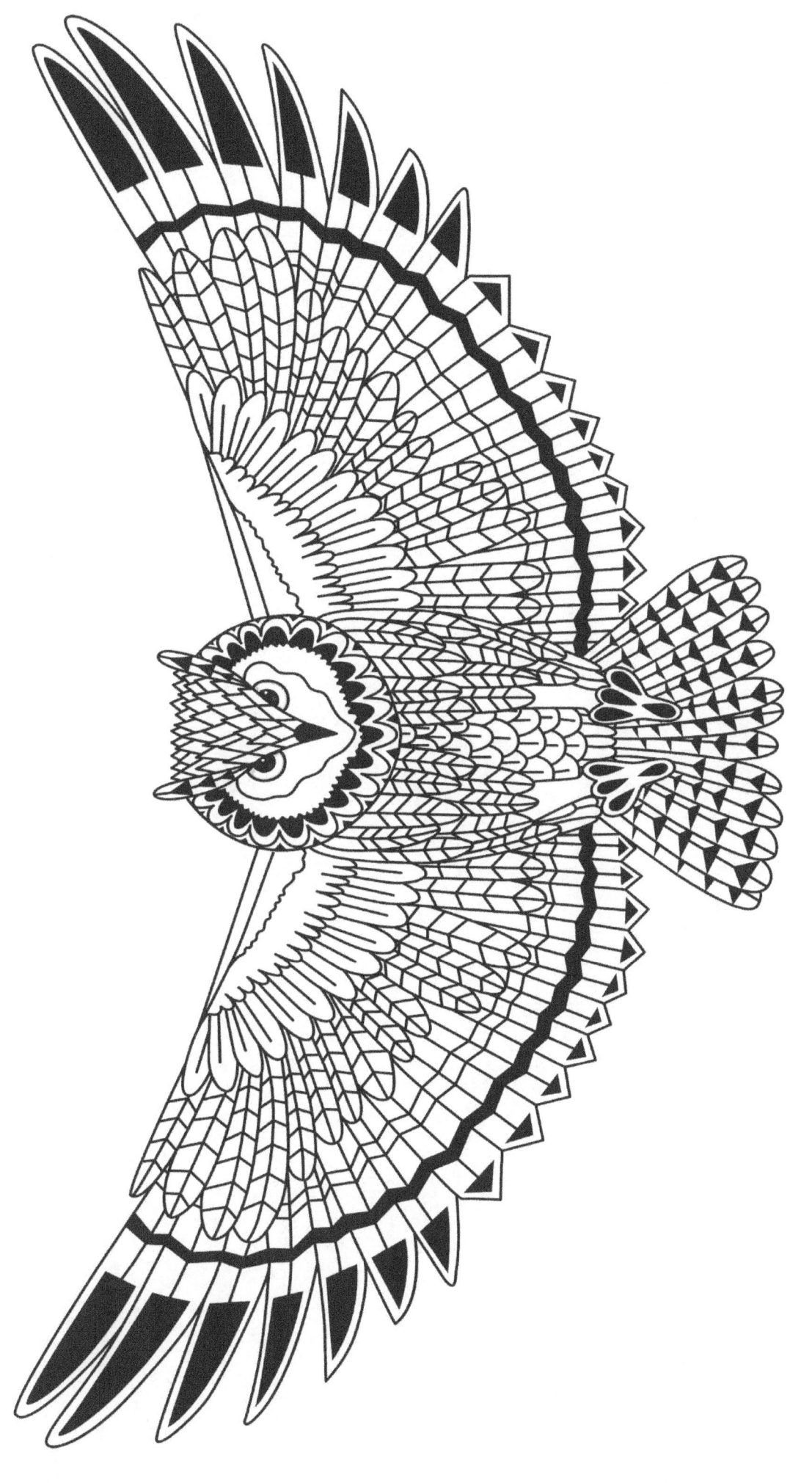

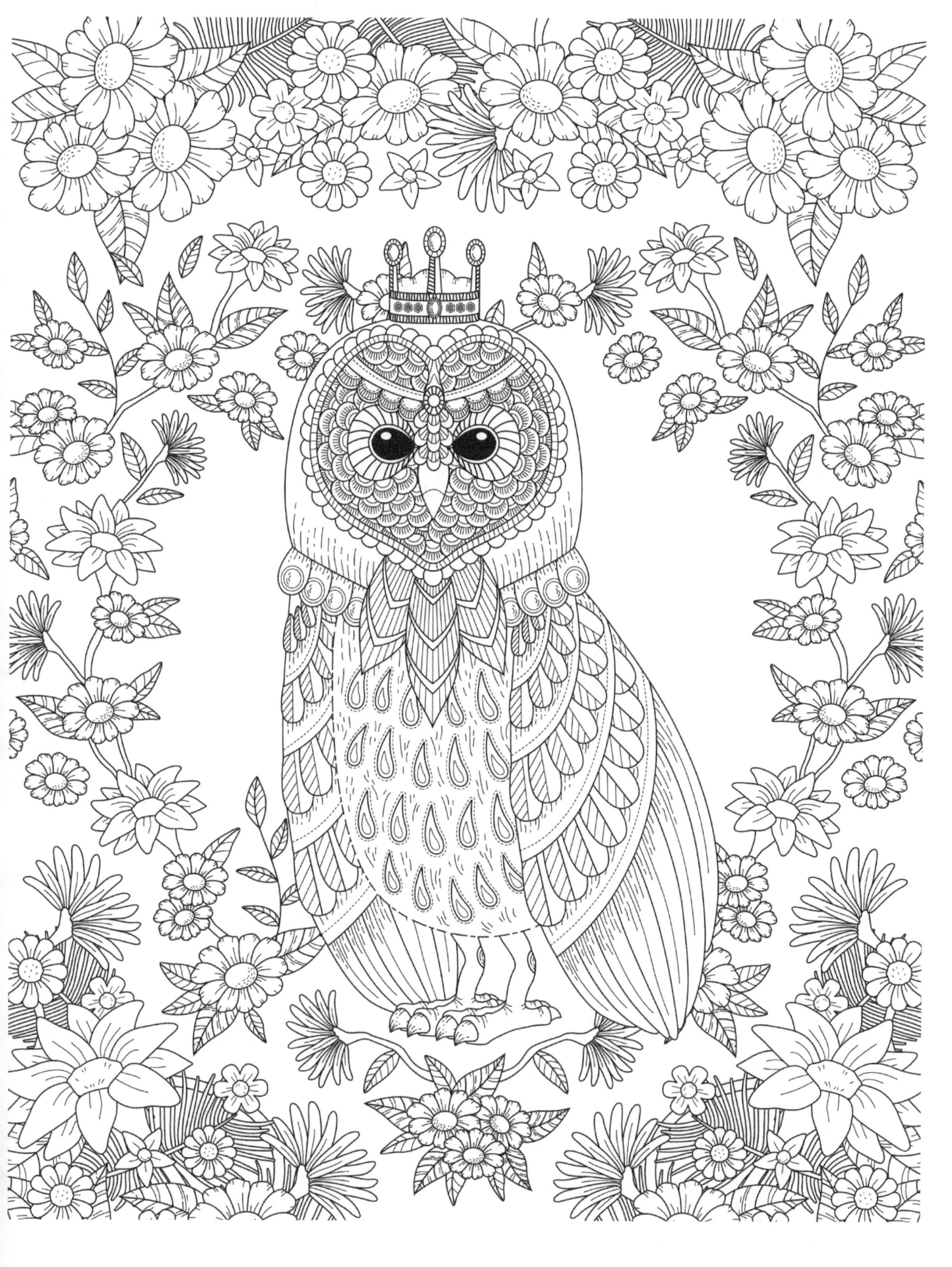

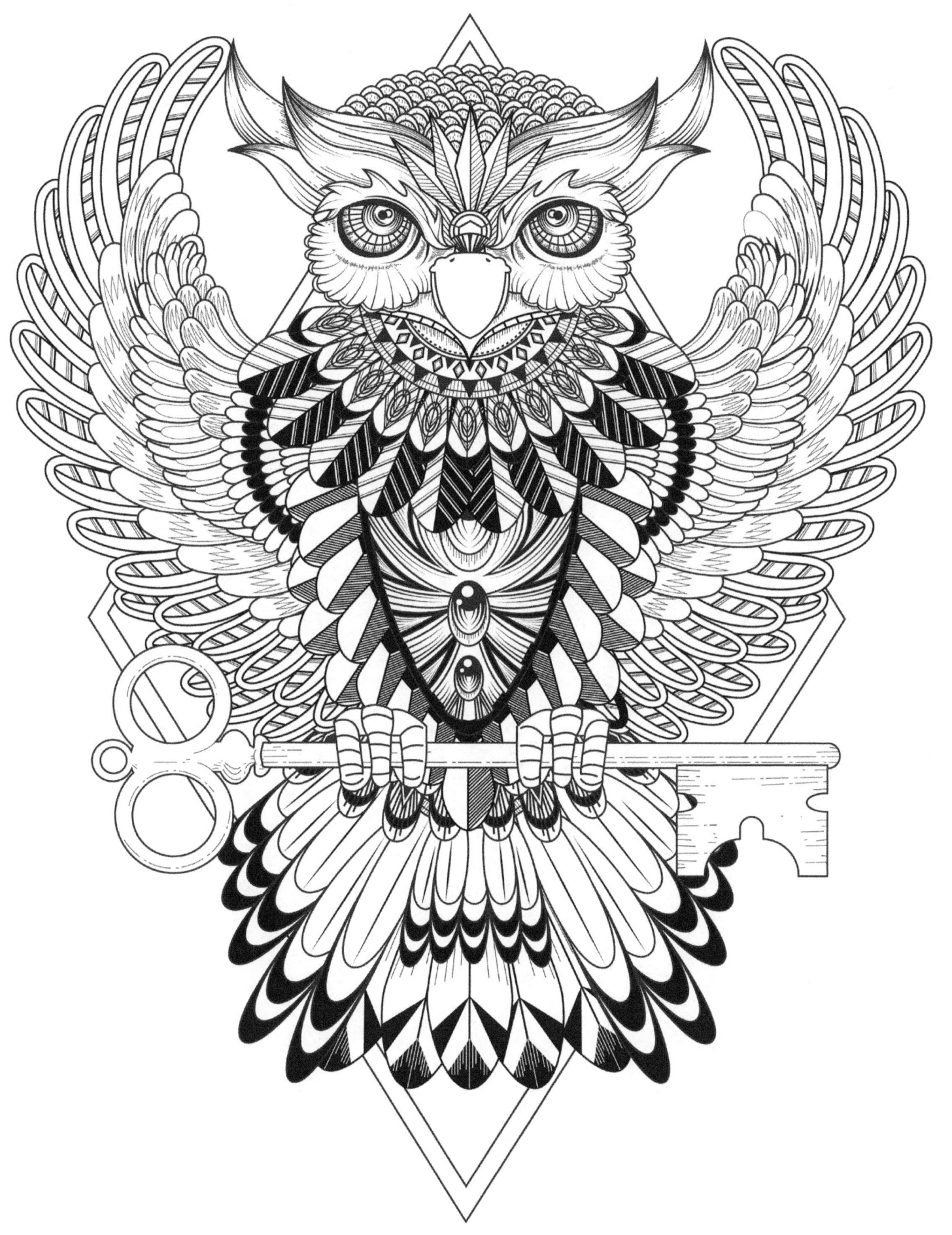

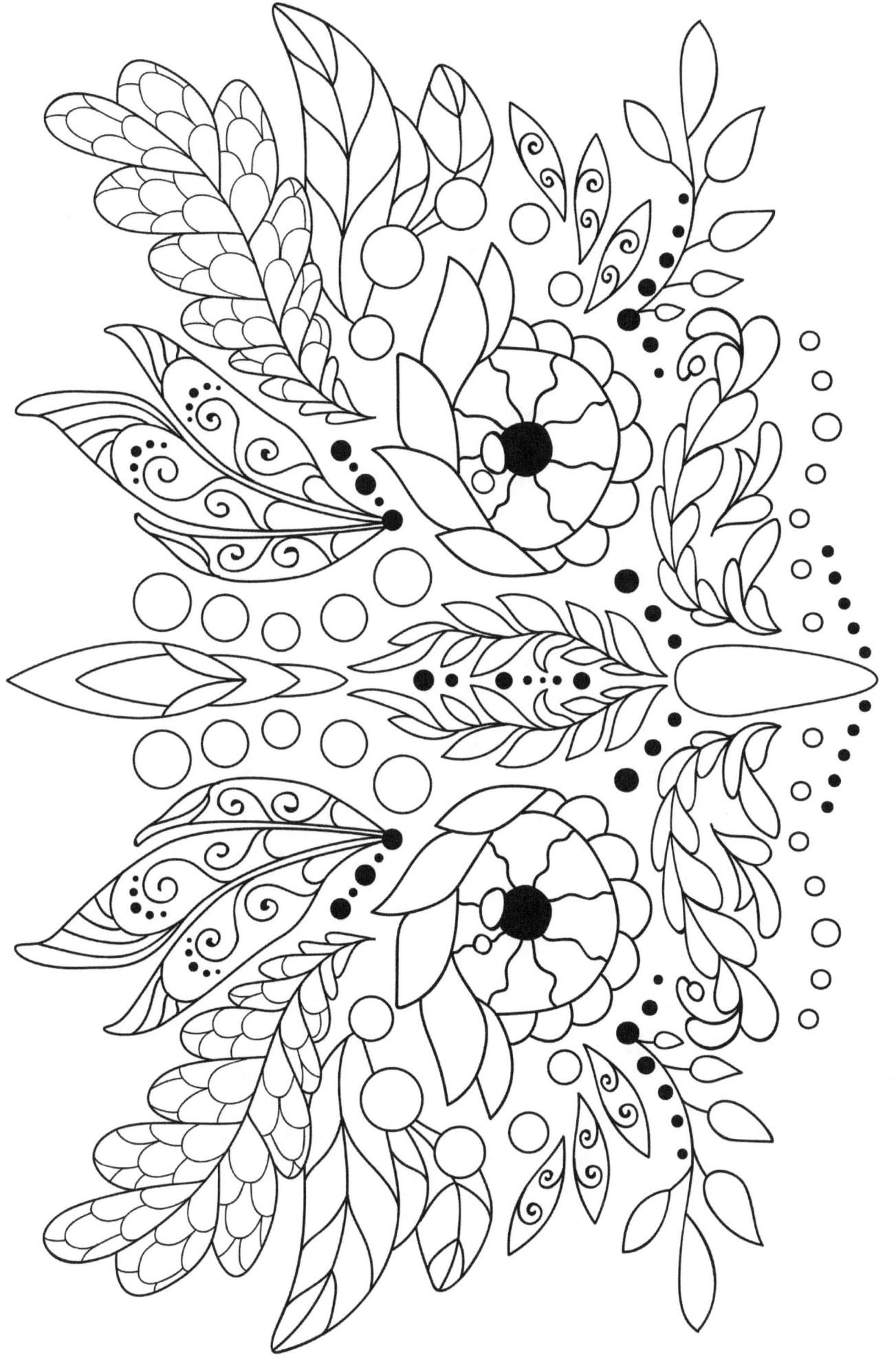

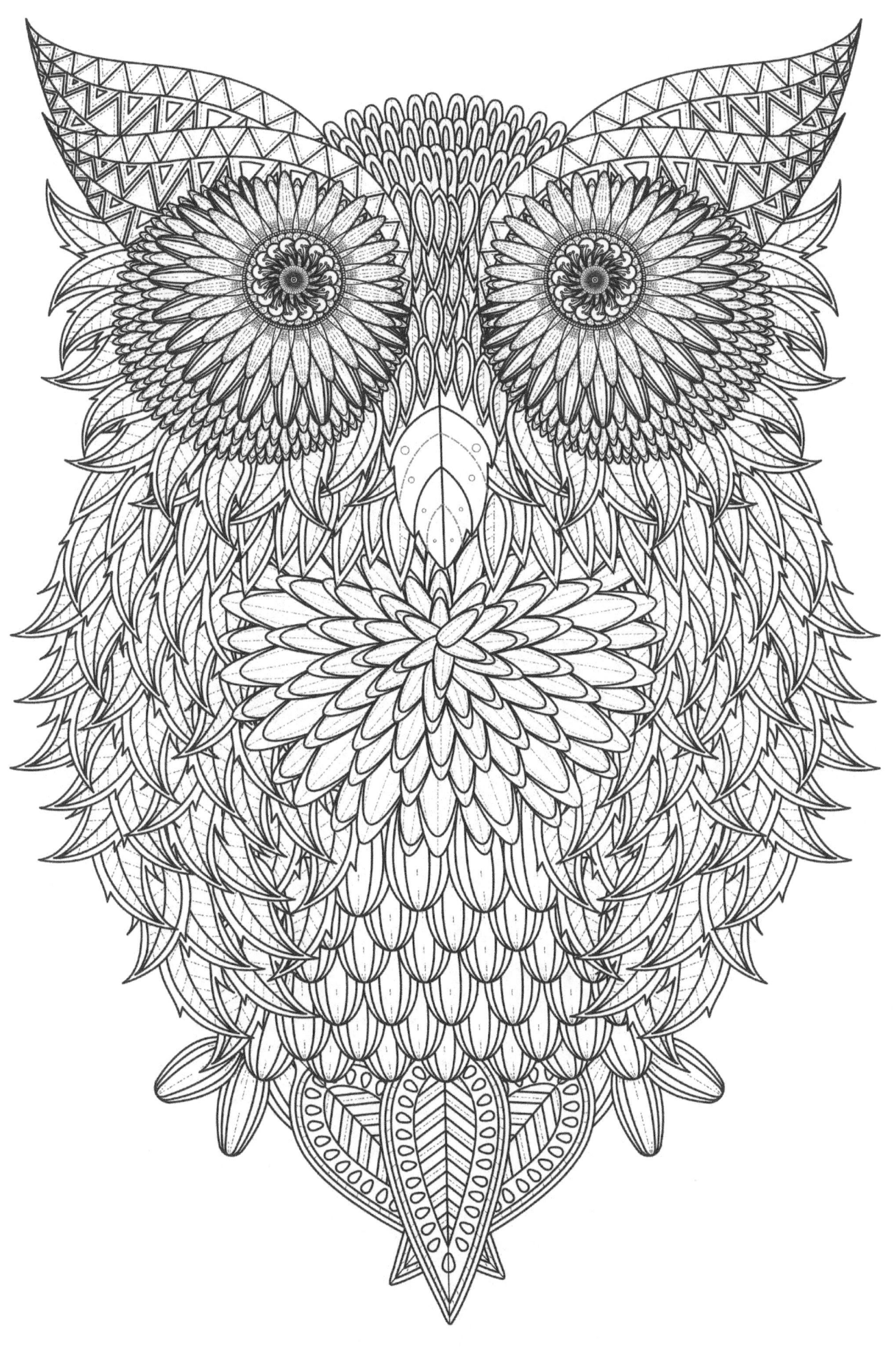

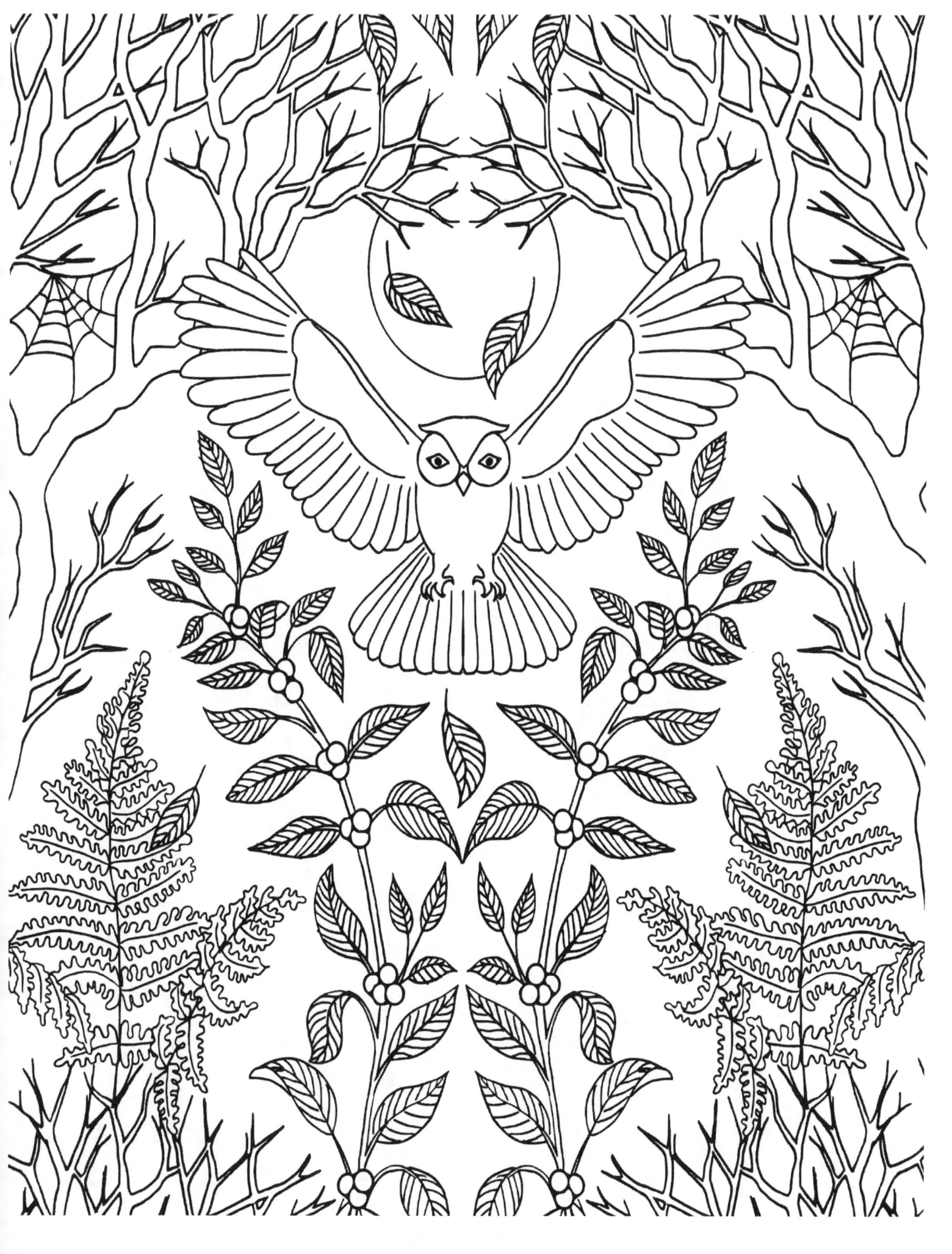

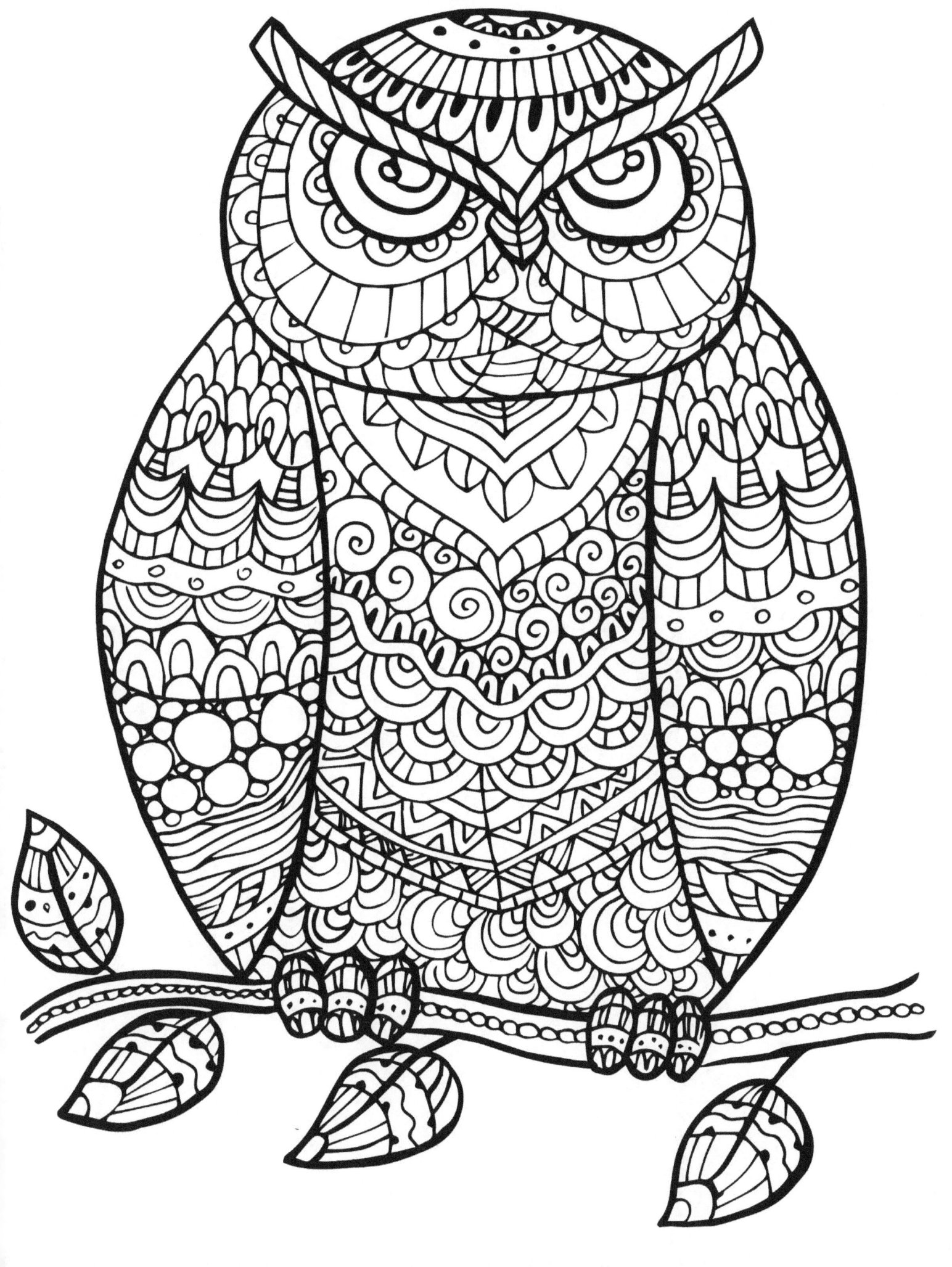

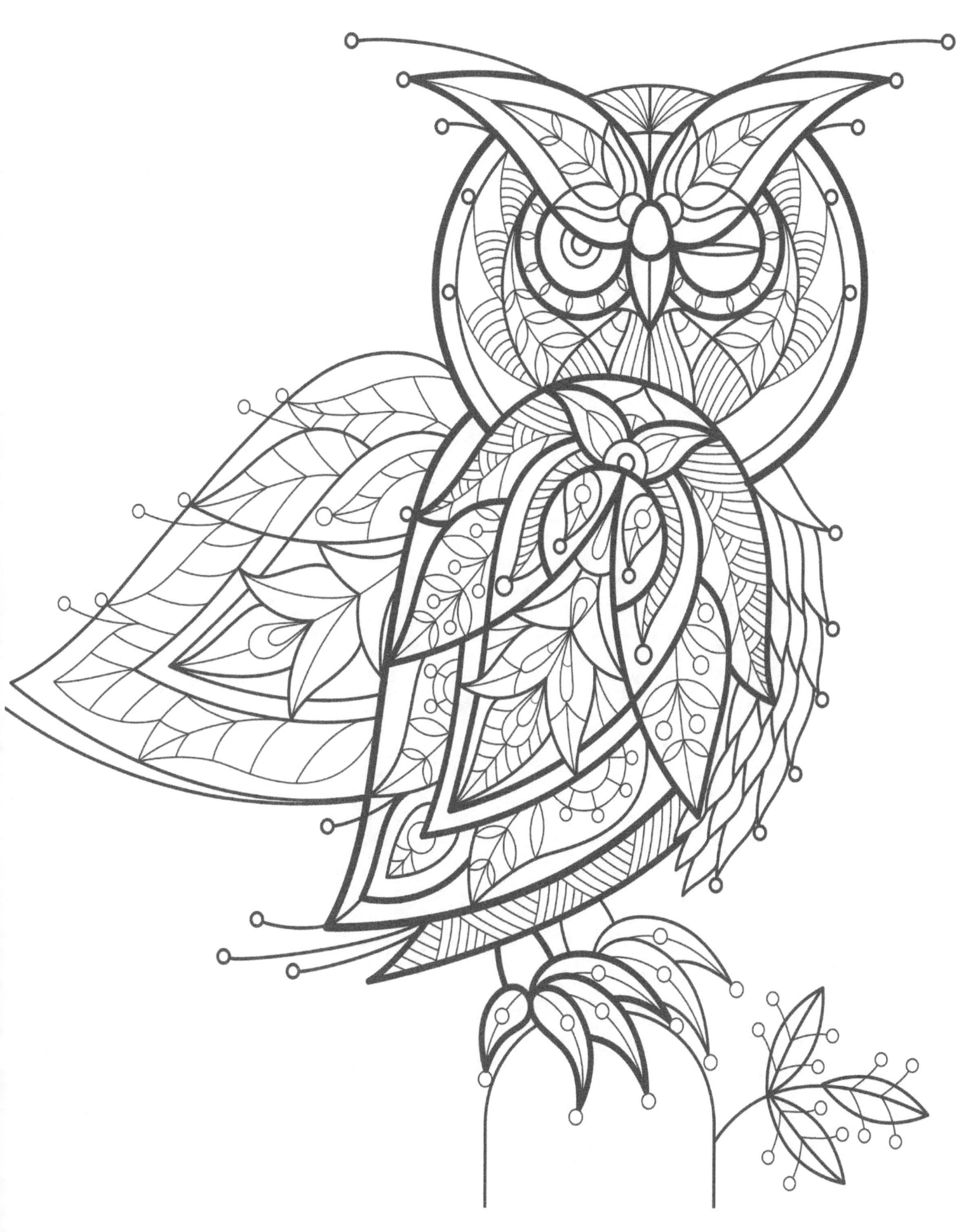

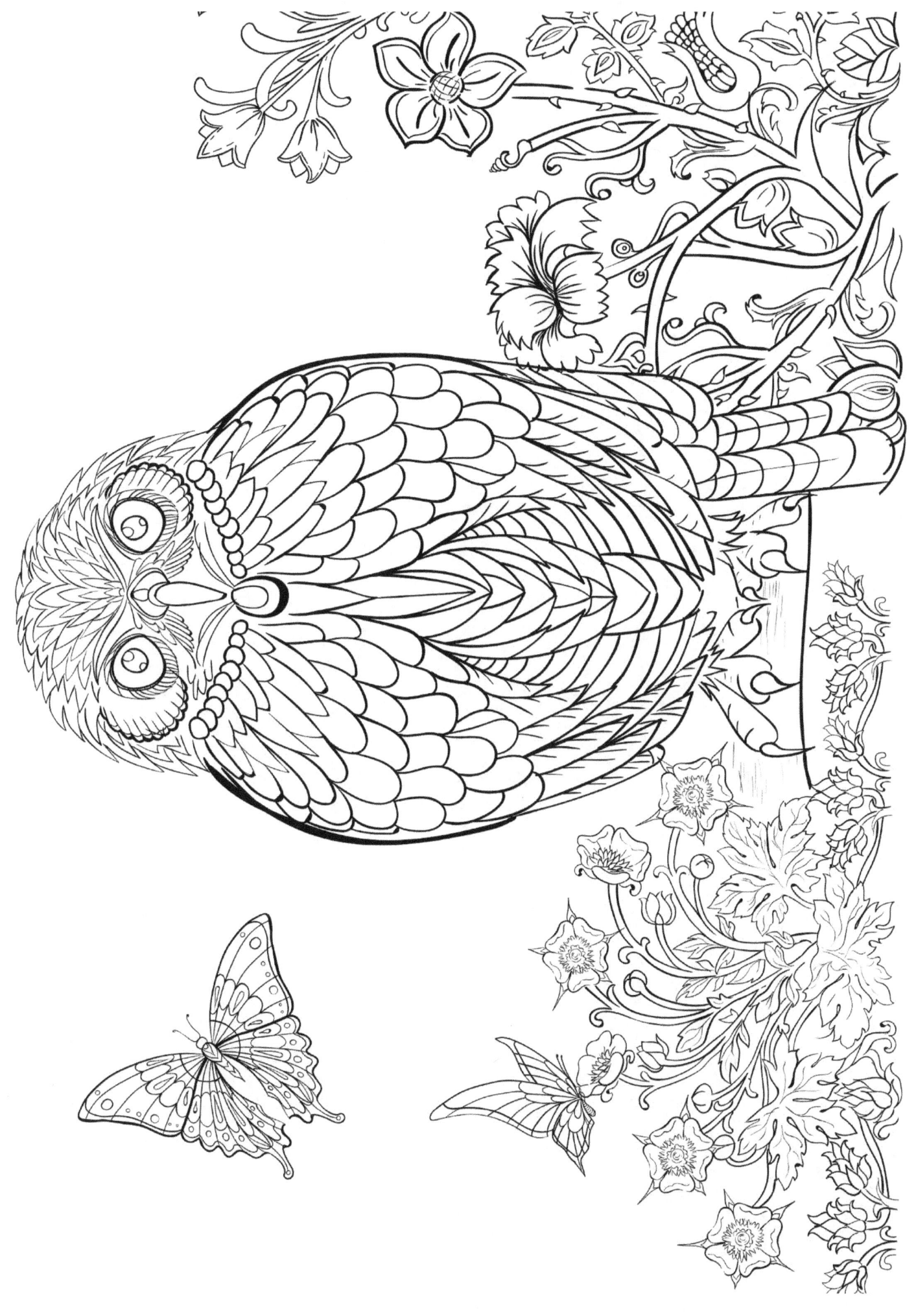

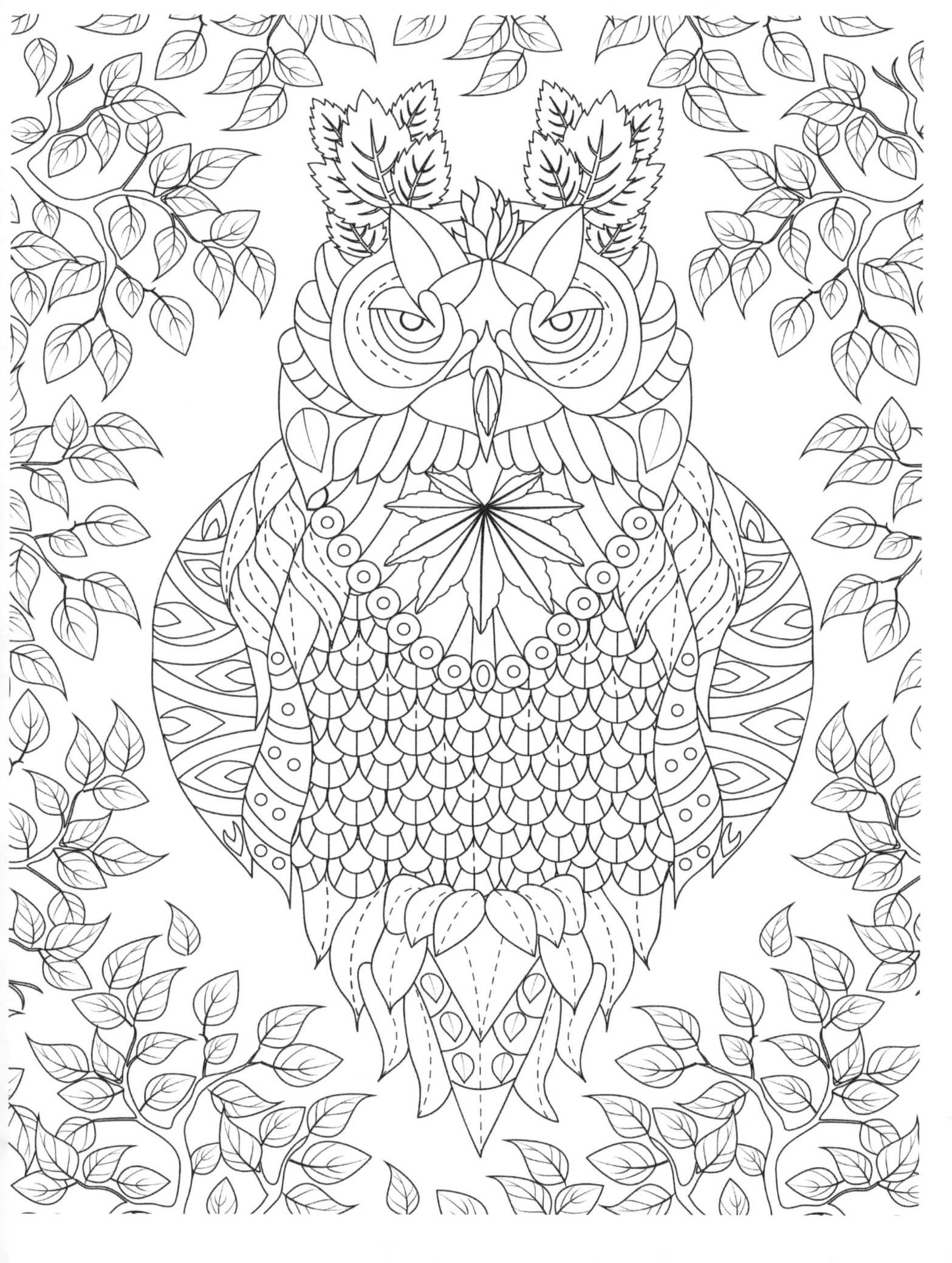

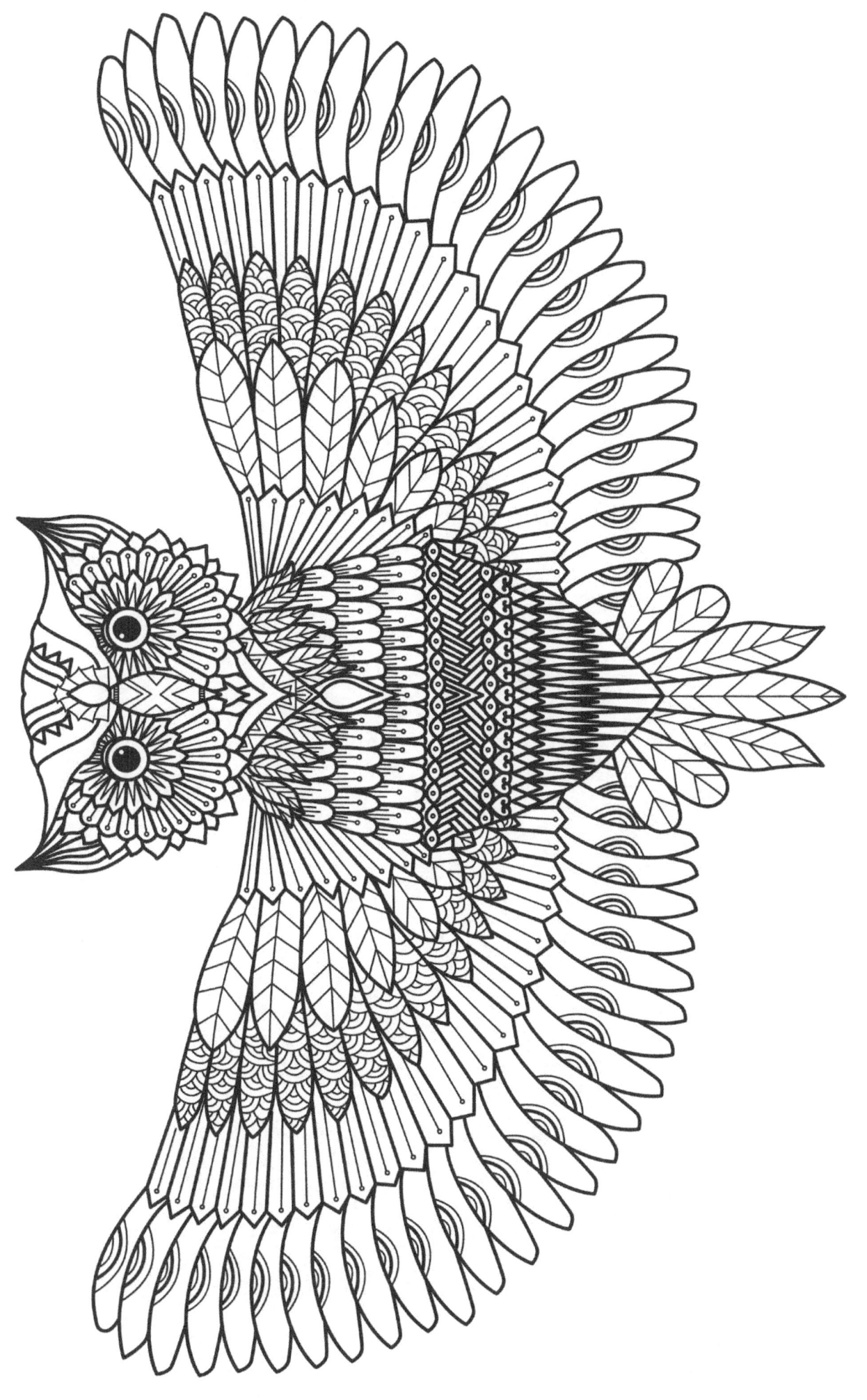

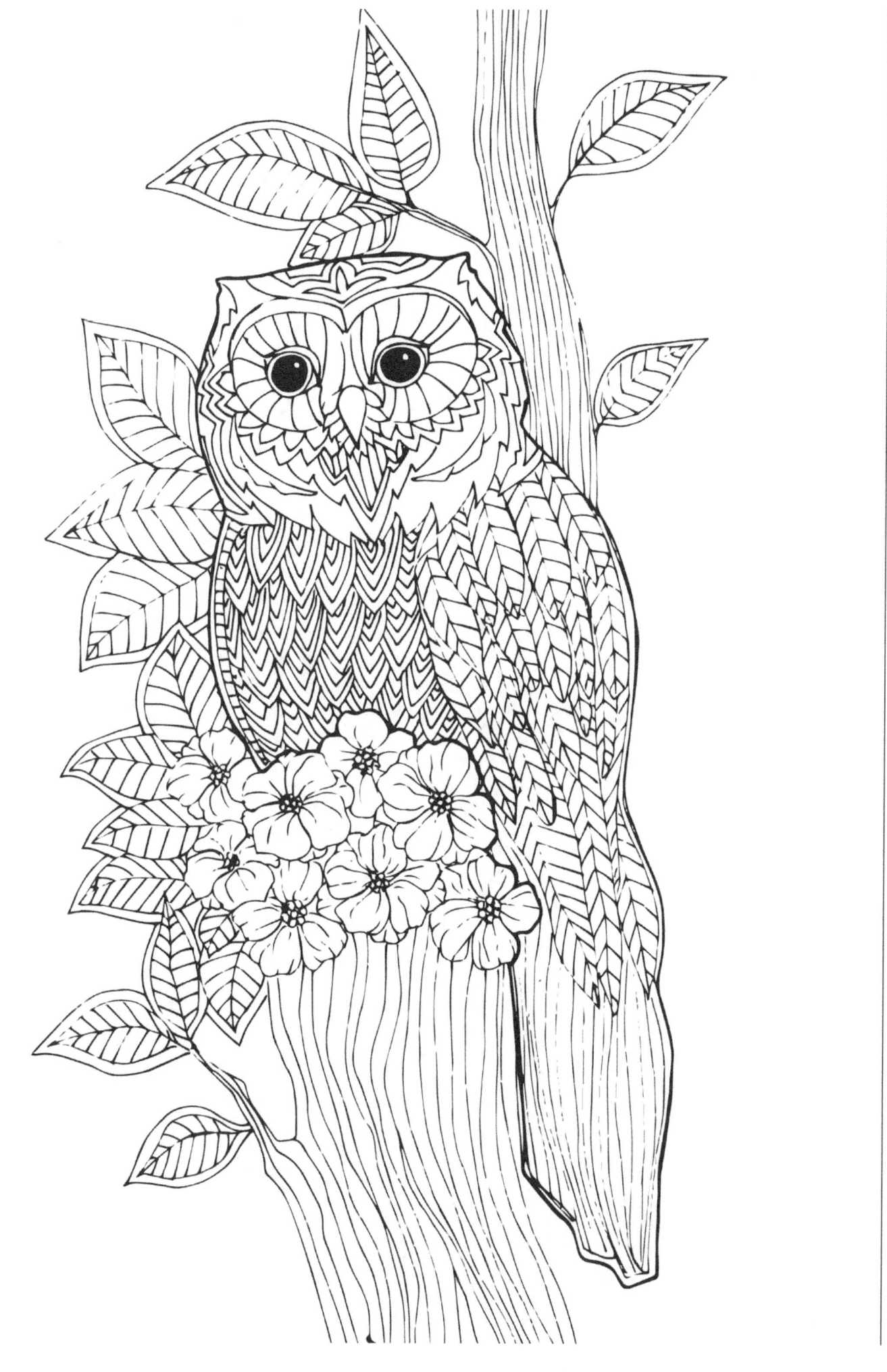

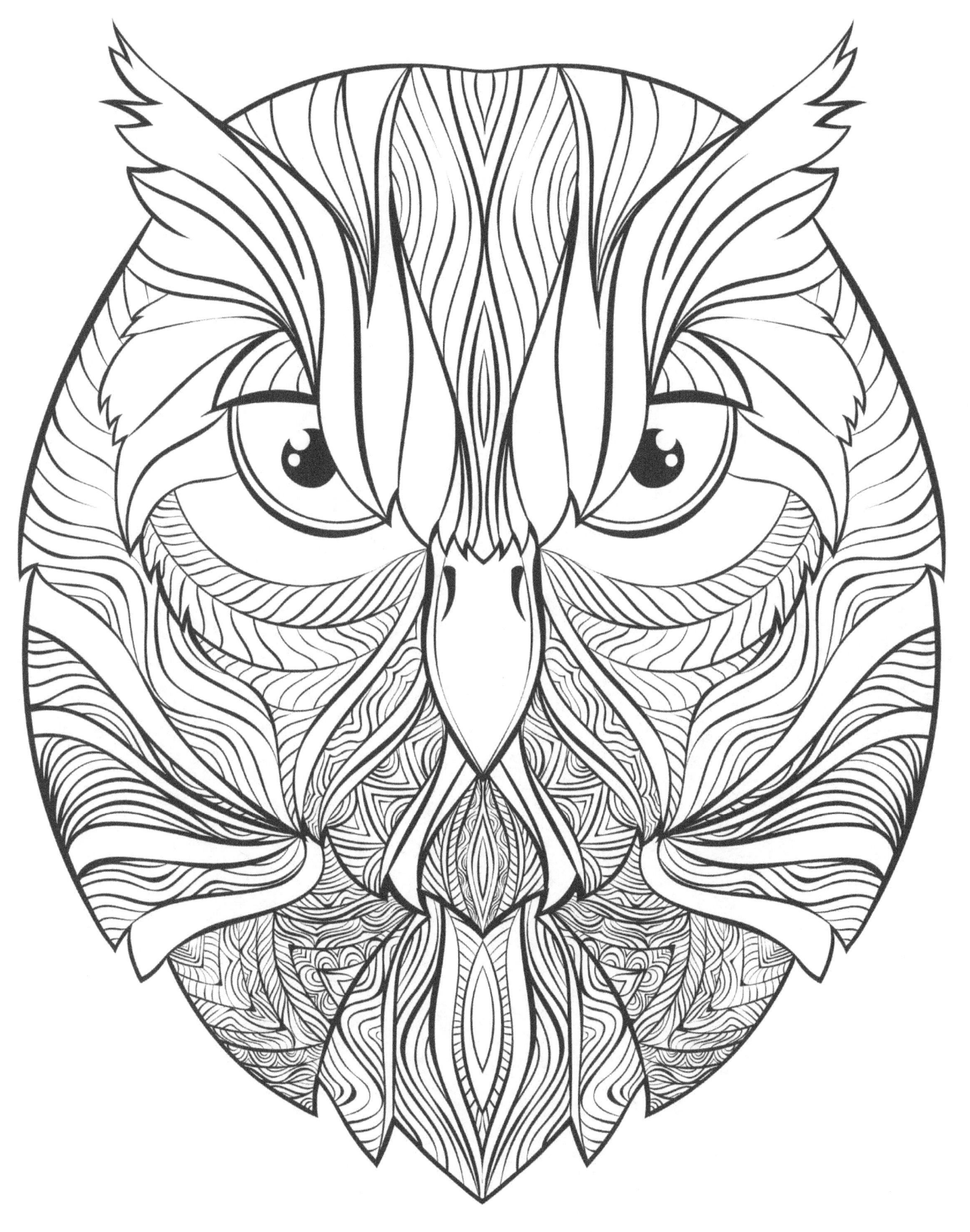

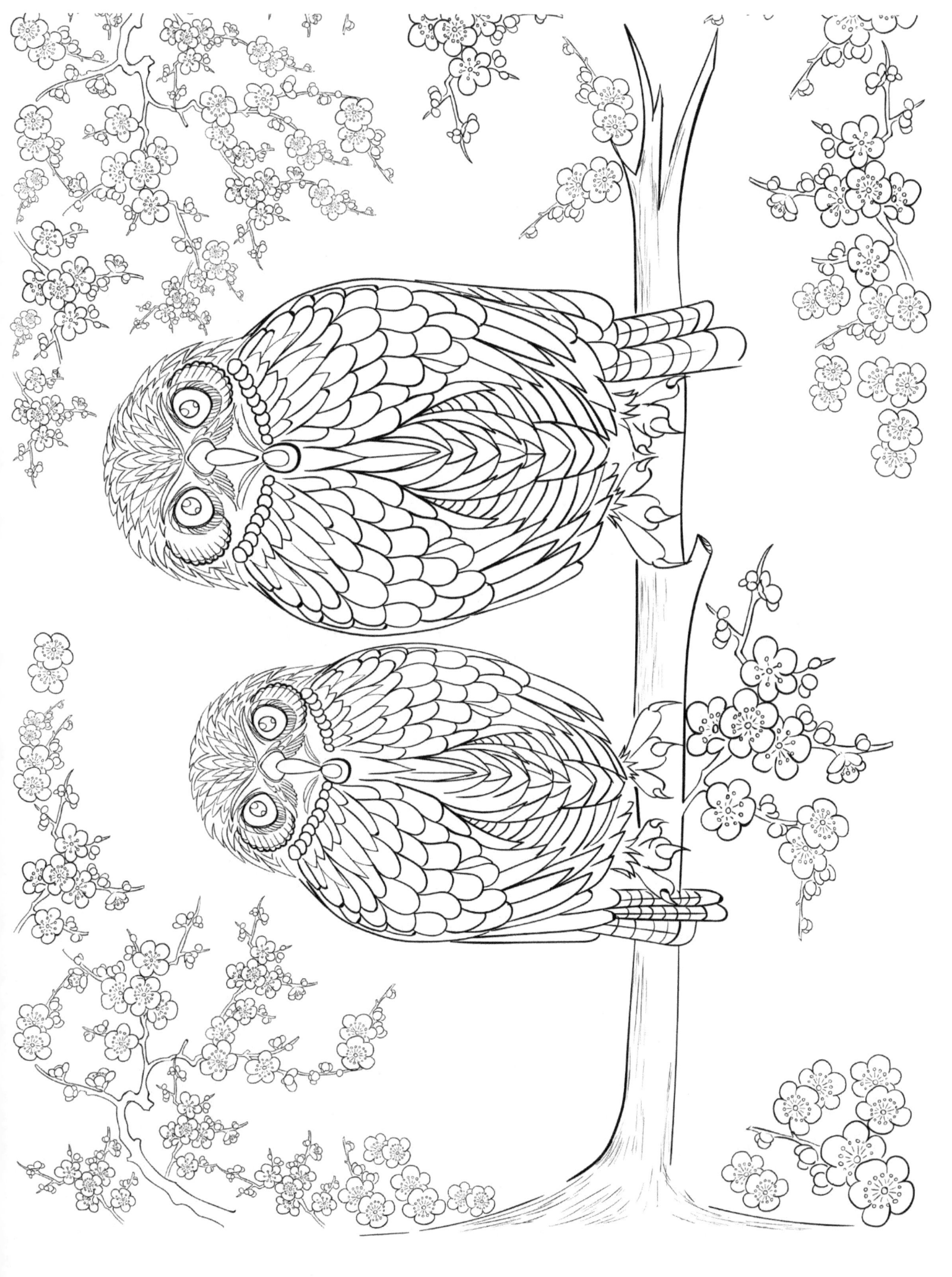

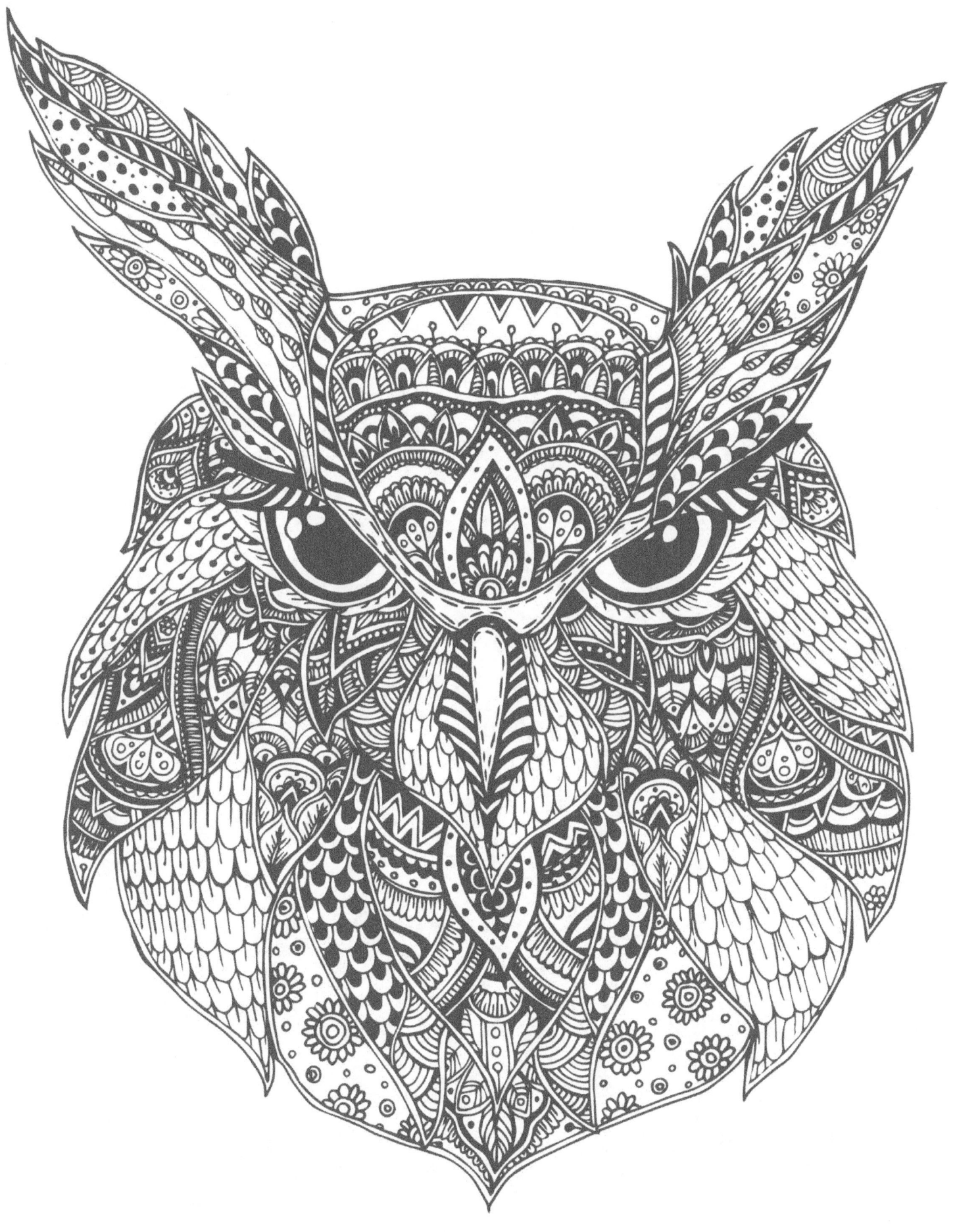

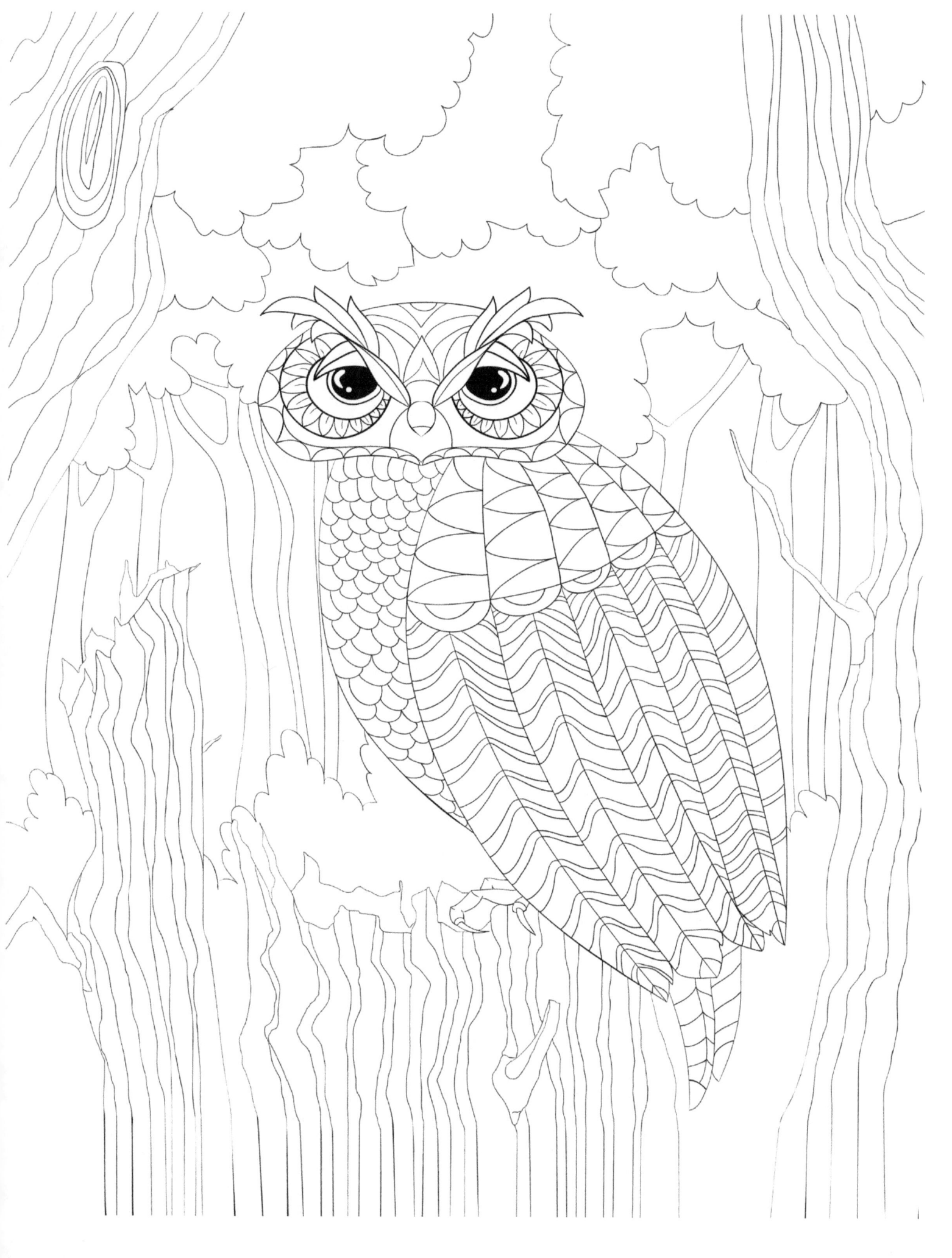

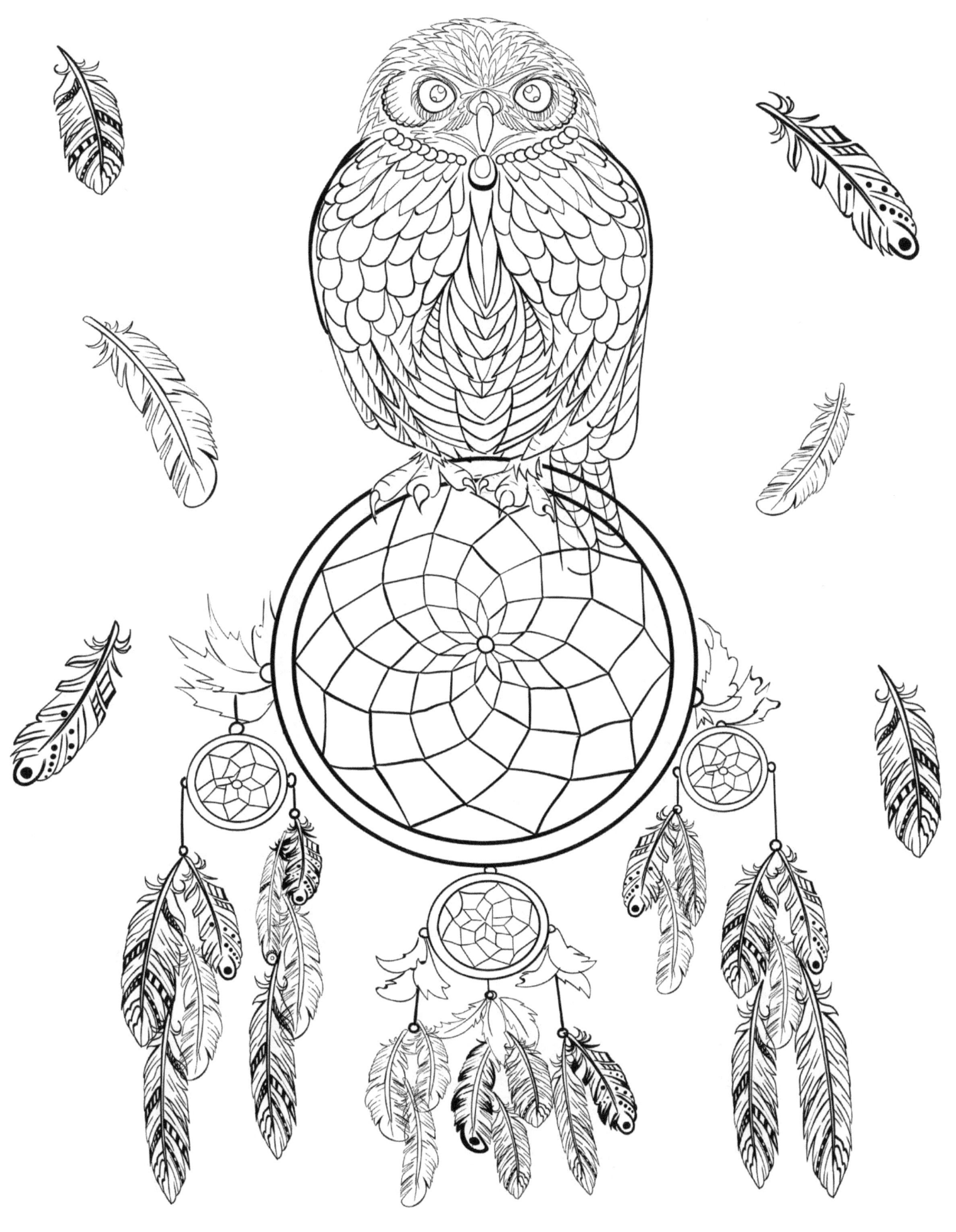

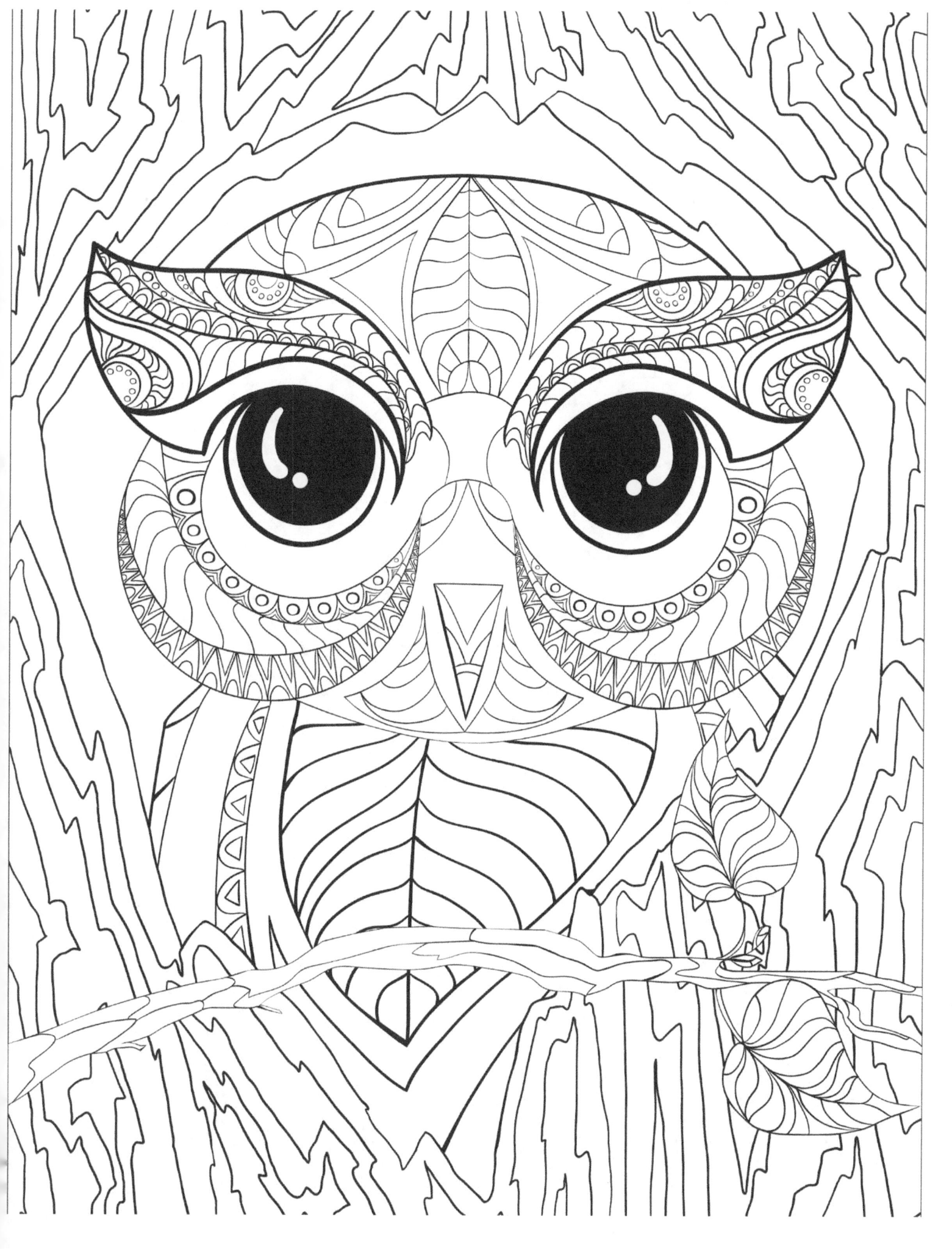

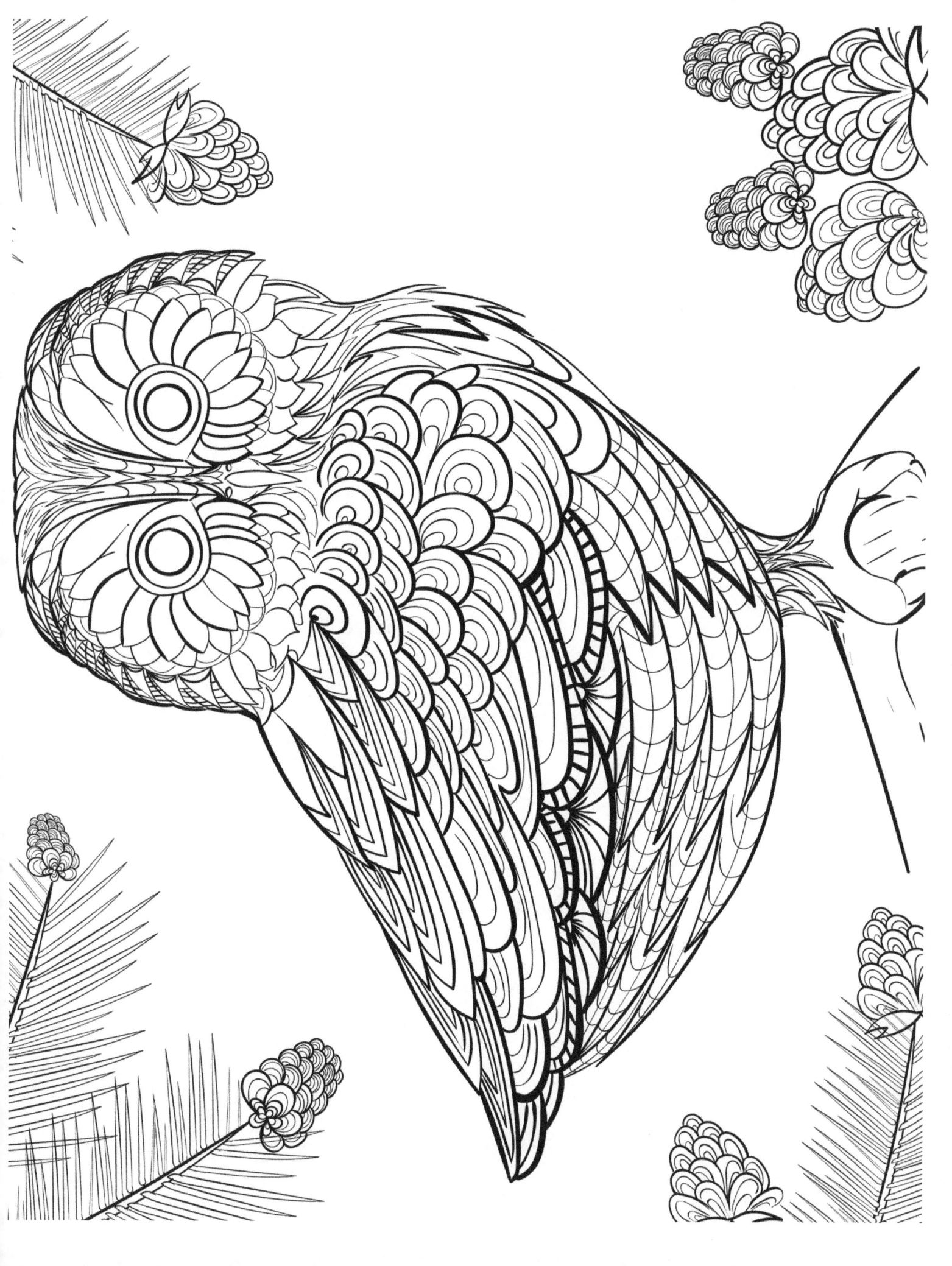

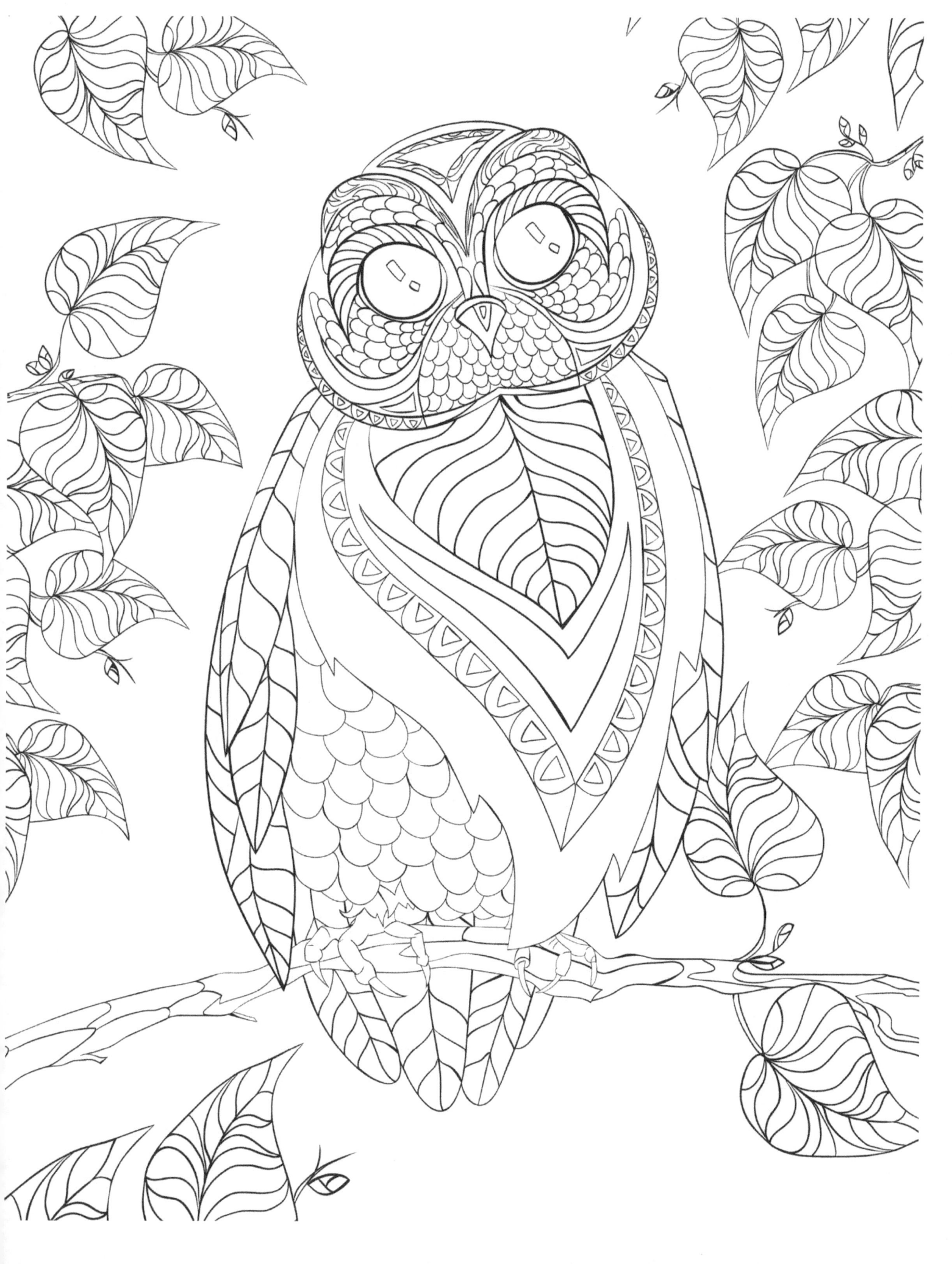

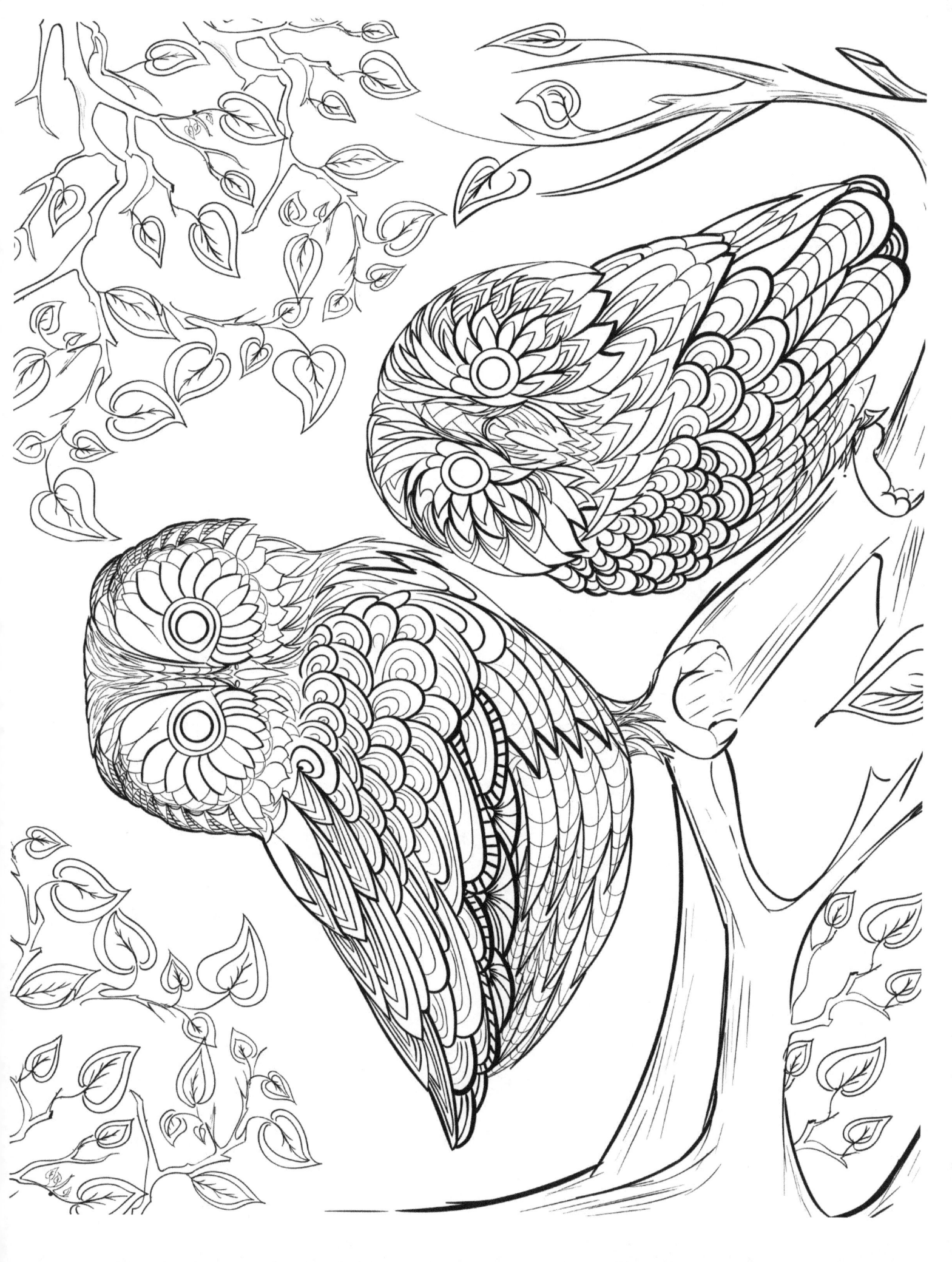

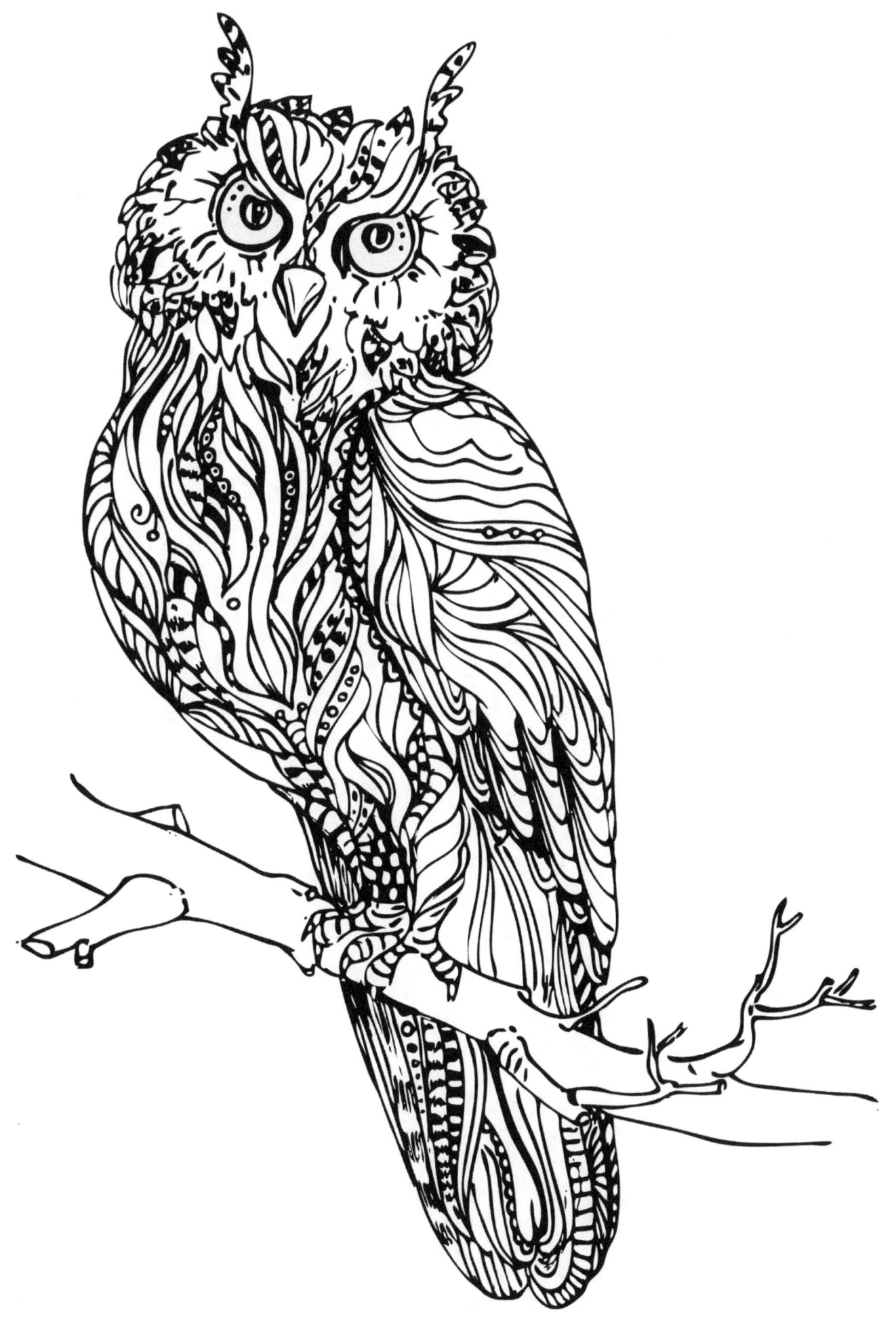

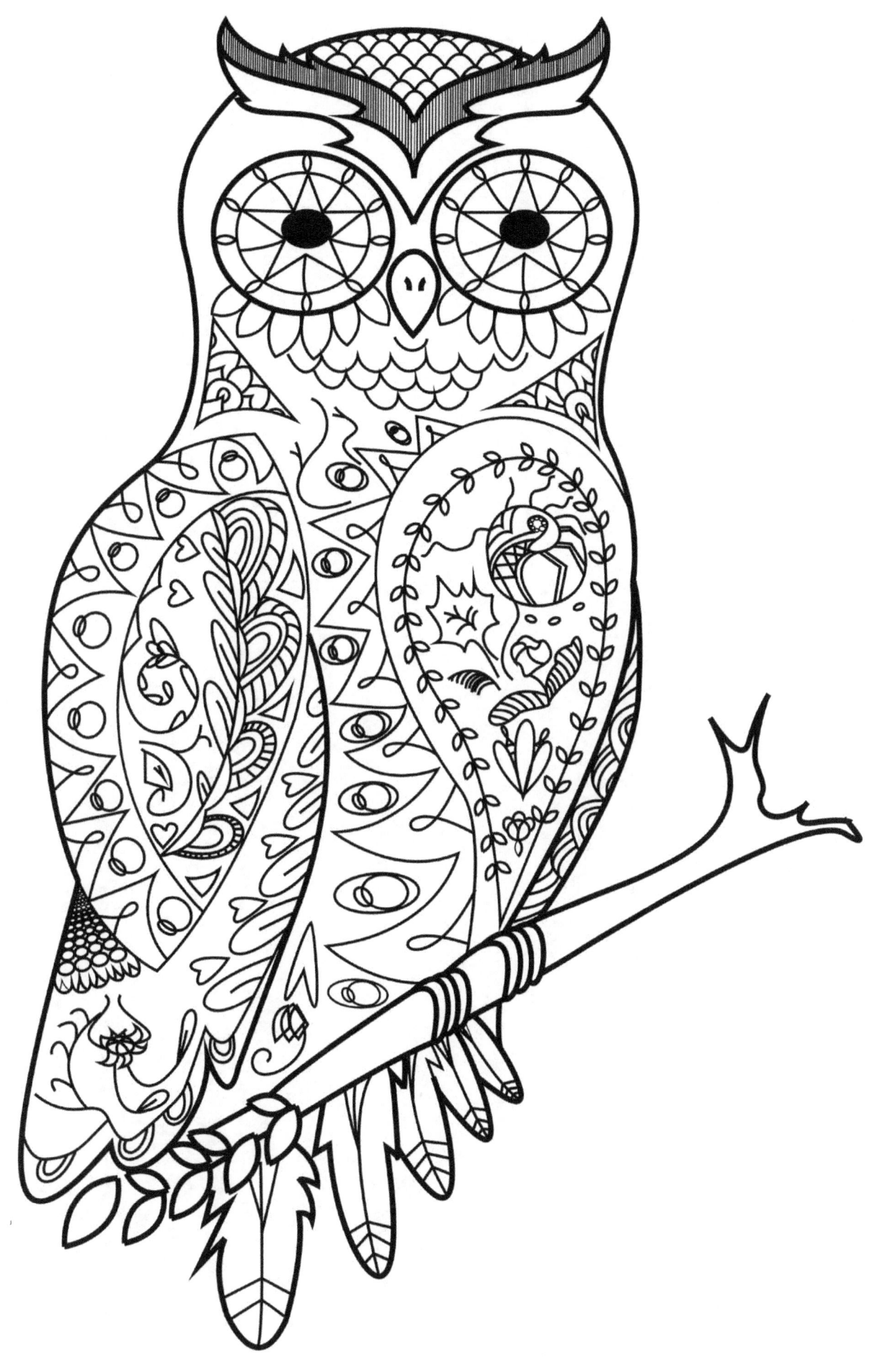

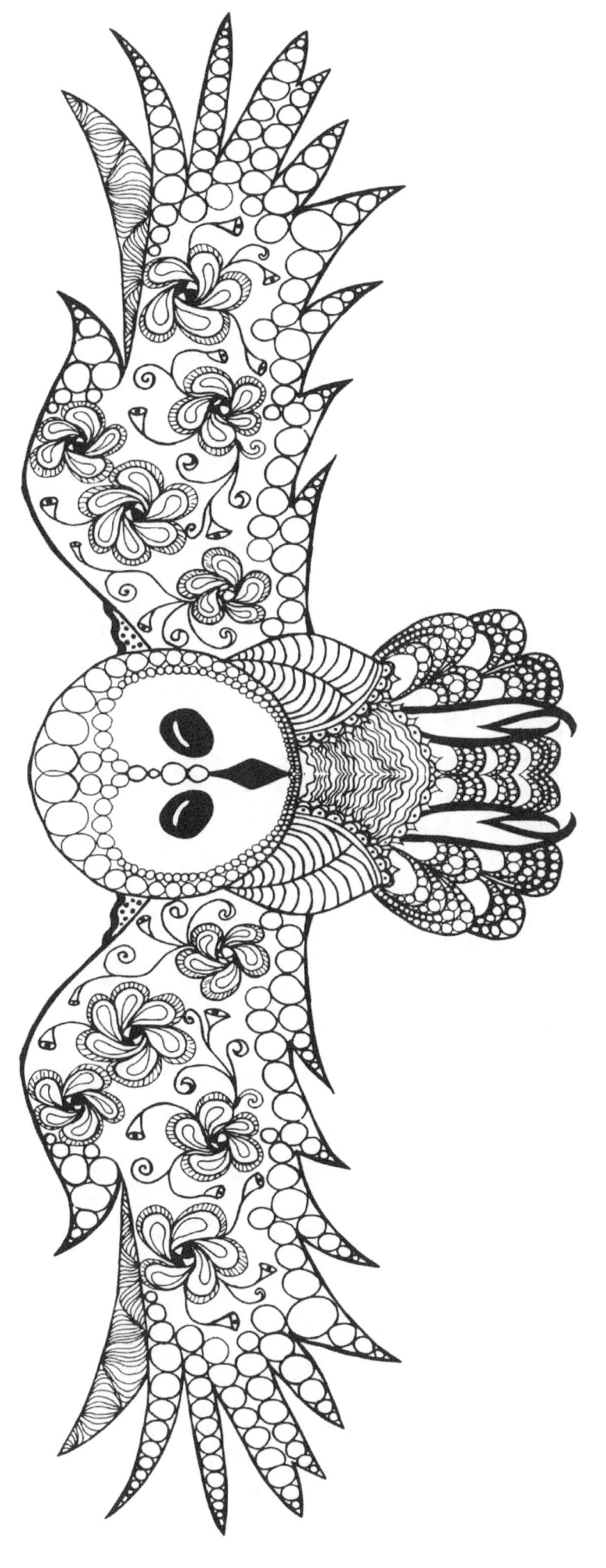

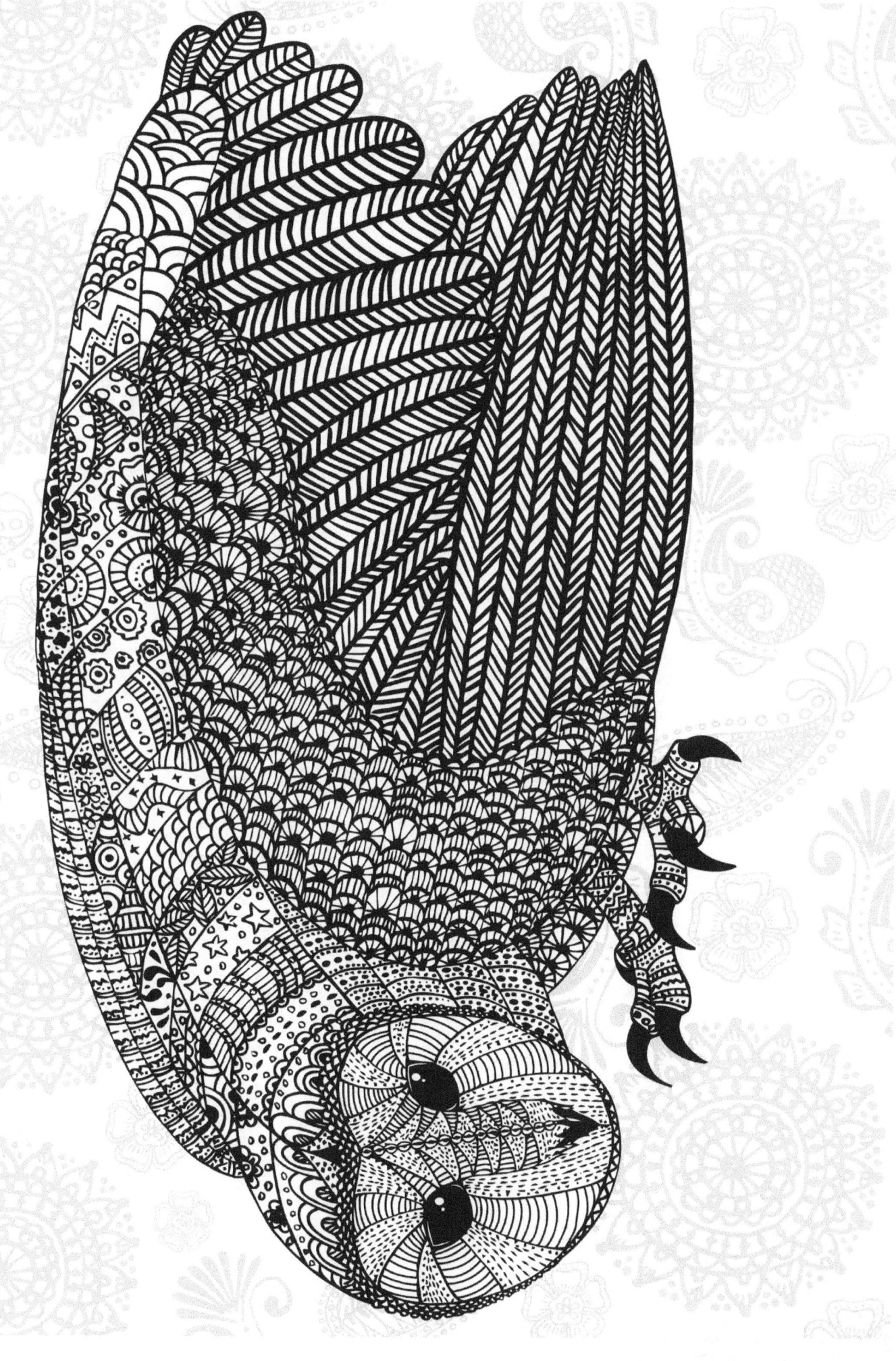

www.ingramcontent.com/pod-product-compliance
Lightning Source LLC
Chambersburg PA
CBHW080709190526
45169CB00006B/2312